D1564874

The Perfect Counselor

A DEVOTIONAL GUIDE ON THE HOLY SPIRIT

By Dr. Johnny Ellison
All Bible References come from the English Standard Version - ESV

Table of Contents

ACKNOWLEDGEMENTS

In the undertaking of this text, my heart has been to bless those who read it and help them to grow in their knowledge of God. In return, those who have been a big help to me have blessed me as well.

I praise God, His son Jesus Christ and the Holy Spirit who have supplied me with an opportunity to be a part of this writing ministry.

I praise God for the Bible, without which I would have nothing to write.

I praise God for my bride being my helpmate and my heartbeat.

I praise God for all three of my children repeatedly telling me that I needed to write a book. The plan is for this to be the first of many.

I praise God for a church family that is encouraging and seeks to allow me the time and opportunity to doing the writing and studying for a project like this.

I praise God for a staff that does so much that it frees up my time to write.

(A special thanks to Suzanne for all of the design, planning, uploading and work involved.)

And, I praise God for the hearts that will be challenged and the lives that will know Jesus better because of this text.

INTRODUCTION

Early in my ministry as a pastor, I was the church planter and pastor of a small congregation that I had planted about two years earlier. I was married, with one child and in my mid-twenties. I had only just begun as a pastor. I was not saved until I was 18 years old, so I was the pastor of a church just a few years after my conversion. I do not recommend this for the average pastor, but this is what God gave me.

One Sunday evening, after a special children's program, I had one of our youth come to me and explain that her uncle was in from out of town and that he needed to speak to me. I told her that was fine, and she went to get him. The gentleman that this young lady brought to me was so obviously in crisis that I could tell as soon as he walked up. His cheeks were sunken in. And, while he was probably around six feet tall, he could not have weighed more than 150-160 pounds – though his frame would suggest that he was naturally a bigger man that that. He had dark circles around his eyes, and a desperate look.

We began to talk some, and I realized that we needed far more than a few minutes at the back of the church. I asked him to come by the next day. He told me that his sister's husband (the sister was the mother of the youth that brought him to me) could drive him there.

The next day this gentleman was brought by my office in our small, neat church campus (one building that seated about 100 with a kitchen, four classrooms and an office) and he sat down across from my desk. He was at least twice my age, though he looked older than that. I asked him to tell me what was going on in his life.

He began by telling me that he lived out of state in the northwest United States. He had dealt with a bi-polar condition most of his life but took medication that kept it under control. He explained that he had a wife and two boys who were back home. He went on to tell me that he had stopped taking his meds, so that he would be able to drink (a person cannot combine those meds and alcohol…so, at least he knew that…). He had become a bi-polar, alcoholic who was off his meds to control his mental health issues. Finally, his wife told him to leave until he could come back as a reasonably normal person.

He explained that he had taken a Greyhound bus from his home to where we were and was staying at his sister's house. He felt like he had ruined his family, and desperately missed his wife and two boys. Then…like a kick in the gut, he said something to me that I will never forget – and that rocked me at that moment. He said,

> "I have a loaded .38 pistol in my suitcase at home. Last night
> I sat on my bed with it in my hand. I was ready to put it in my
> mouth and pull the trigger. I did not do that, because I thought
> that you might have something to say to me that might make
> a difference today."

There was silence for a few moments, and I hoped he could not hear the "THUD!" in my stomach or my knees shaking as I sat at my desk. At that moment, I was glad I decided not to come around my desk and sit beside him, or he might have heard me gulp.

I remember thinking, "I have no idea what to do here." It was a crisis moment for a 25-year-old pastor, and I was scared that I might steer him wrong.

I had founded my ministry and my role as a pastor on the authority of God's Word. I knew that the reality of Scripture was an anchor, and so I took this gentleman to the Scriptures and explained what it meant to be born again. Right there in my office he prayed to repent and turn to Christ as his Savior. I believe he was born-again at that moment, but that was only the beginning.

For the next three weeks, he committed to being at every church service in addition to meeting with me two days per week. In those meetings, I began to walk him through the Bible to show him what happened when he was saved.

After a few weeks, we met only once a week, but I still walked him through the Bible. I began to show him how he could learn to rely on God and the Holy Spirit of God for direction, help, power and guidance. After a couple of months of meeting like that, we stopped but he continued consistently being in church. Just over a year later he began to serve in multiple ways at that church. Several years after that he was asked to come serve a position at another church in youth ministry.

I remember being astounded at that man's life and seeing first-hand early in my ministry how the Holy Spirit of God was really the Perfect Counselor for us all. I certainly do not suggest that trained and licensed counselors are not necessary many times, but I learned then that The Perfect Counselor is ultimately who helps God's children.

As you work through this devotional book, you can use it one of three ways – or all three.

1. As a daily devotional for your quiet time to gain more insight into what God's Word says about the Holy Spirit in your life.
2. As a devotional but also a study guide to prepare and listen to the series of messages I preached at Golden Acres Baptist titled The Perfect Counselor.
3. As a small group study using the questions as a study guide at the end of each chapter/week.

However you use this text, it is my prayer that you would finish it with a much greater understanding of what it means to walk with God with the help of His Holy Spirit - The Perfect Counselor. May you walk in His power and His presence!

God Bless,
Pastor Johnny Ellison
Colossians 3:3-4

THE PERFECT COUNSELOR DEVOTIONS: WEEK 1
Alone with God

DAY 1: His Early Work

Genesis 1:1-2

"In the beginning, God created the heavens and the earth. The earth was without form and void, and darkness was over the face of the deep. And the Spirit of God was hovering over the face of the waters."

"In the beginning…"

God did not actually begin at some point in history. He is eternal and has always been. The Scriptures, in this context, use "In the beginning…" as a statement referencing the eternality of God the Father.

And, in the context of the eternality of God the Father, so is the eternality of the Holy Spirit ("And the Spirit of God was hovering over the face of the waters."). In the same way that God the Father is eternal, so is God the Son ("In the beginning was the Word…and the Word became flesh…" John 1:1a, 14a) and God the Holy Spirit.

Imagine that…? The Holy Spirit precedes every circumstance you or I have ever faced. The Holy Spirit preceded every circumstance the Apostle Paul, Peter, John, James or Andrew would ever face.

The Holy Spirit preceded every challenge Mary, Joseph, Zacharias or Elisabeth faced.

The Holy Spirit preceded Malachi, Amos, Jeremiah, Isaiah and Ezekiel and all of the challenging sermons they ever preached.

The Holy Spirit preceded Ezra, Nehemiah, Esther, Daniel, Shadrach, Meshach and Abednego and the great courage they displayed.

The Holy Spirit preceded Solomon, David, Saul, Samson, Gideon, Elijah, Elisha and all the twelve tribes of Israel as they faced the challenge of overcoming their enemies versus the nation Israel.

Before Joshua, Moses, Joseph, Jacob, Rebekah, Isaac, Sarah, Abraham or Noah faced heart break, victory, disappointment and spiritual gain, the Holy Spirit was present.

And…even before Job, Enoch, Adam and Eve faced the challenges and pitfalls of a world increasingly wrought by sin, the Holy Spirit was there.

And…if the Holy Spirit preceded these, how much more has the Holy Spirit preceded you? How much more has the Holy Spirit preceded the heartache you faced yesterday or the uncertainty of today?

Because the Holy Spirit, who is fully God and all of God in the third person, was where you are before you got there, He has answers, help, comfort, solutions and victory about which you have yet to consider. Because the Holy Spirit preceded your challenge or victory long before you arrived, His solutions are already worked out for you.

You never know what a day holds but know that a day which provides you a shocking challenge, turn of events or unexpected trial was already inhabited by the eternal One. He is there to walk with you, advise you, direct you and empower you.

The eternality of the Holy Spirit is not just that He was always there from the beginning, but that He will also always be there ahead of us…and is there already in our future.

FINAL THOUGHT: Spend time daily thinking on and seeking leadership from the Holy Spirit from His Word and conversation in prayer. HE KNOWS WHAT YOU NEED!

DAY 2: In Whom is the Spirit of God?
Genesis 41:37-38
"This proposal pleased Pharaoh and all his servants. And Pharaoh said to his servants, 'Can we find a man like this, in whom is the Spirit of God?'"

What kind of person is sought out in an entire kingdom? When the Pharaoh asked this question, he was the emperor of the most powerful kingdom and empire on earth. He was looking for one man. The single qualification of this man was "in whom is the Spirit of God..." A man exhibiting the Spirit of God was most critical to the most powerful ruler on earth. A man exhibiting the Spirit of God was most critical to the pagan ruler of a pagan empire.

Exhibiting the Spirit of God must produce such a distinct lifestyle that it stands out among all the people who lived in a massive nation (including the slaves and prisoners – which Joseph was) like Egypt. If the life lived by the power of God's Spirit is so distinct that it stands out in a far flung, paganistic, Pharaoh worshipping, slave owning nation like ancient Egypt, then it likely stands out among any nation, any people and any culture that exists even on earth today.

On April 20, 1999, two gunmen entered the halls of Columbine High School in Littleton, Colorado. In what was a horrible, senseless and callous murder of thirteen people, some stories of courage and faith emerged. One of those stories involved students being killed who affirmed their faith in the face of the shooters. After the horrible and chaotic day, there were varying reports of who actually stood (though Cassie Bernall was the most well-known and publicized of the teen martyrs) in the face of horror. These stories were so powerful, in an American culture inundated by information, that they became national news stories. These students did something so counter-culture that all of America – and the world – heard about it.

God is probably not calling you to gain the attention of the culture by dying for your faith but living by the power of His Holy Spirit will cause such a distinct lifestyle in you that the culture around you will sit up and take notice. Young Joseph was merely a prisoner and slave in a vast empire, and yet the Pharaoh – essentially the king of the universe at that time – took notice because of the working of God's Spirit in his life.

—

Galatians 5:22-23 lists the characteristics of a life empowered by the Holy Spirit of God. These characteristics are so distinct and so unique that they stand out in the climate of the current culture. In fact, these characteristics stand out so much that even the most informational, social media driven, and sensational news saturated environment would take notice. If Pharaoh would notice a slave prisoner filled with the Spirit of God, how much more will people notice you as you are filled and empowered with the Spirit of God?

CAN WE FIND A PERSON LIKE THIS...IN WHOM IS THE SPIRIT OF GOD?!

FINAL THOUGHT: For starters, when you are one in whom is Spirit of God your life will look like this:
- Galatians 5:22-23
- Ephesians 4:1-3; 5:18-21
- Colossians 3:12-17

DAY 3: Dance with the One You Brought.
Job 33:1-4
"But now, hear my speech, O Job, and listen to all my words. Behold,
I open my mouth; the tongue in my mouth speaks. My words declare the
uprightness of my heart, and what my lips know they speak sincerely. The
Spirit of God has made me, and the breath of the Almighty gives me life."

Though Elihu was issuing judgment on Job with a self-righteous motive, his basic ideas and thoughts about his existence and ability to live were accurate. Everything he was, and would be, was given Him by the Holy Spirit of God – and Elihu acknowledged this. God's Spirit and God's breath were the reasons for his creation and ongoing life. Even Elihu understood that his very existence and daily walk were enabled by the Spirit of God.

"Always dance with the one you brought." This is a wise piece of sports analysis that speaks to teams that make it to championship games. In those championship games, be it baseball, football, basketball, golf or soccer, sometimes teams will attempt to change the way they play because of the pressure of a big game. Nothing could be more of a mistake for a championship caliber team than to do anything differently than the very approach that helped them get to the final game. In other words, what made your team successful in the beginning is what will make your team successful all the way until the end.

And so it is for God's people. At the conversion of any believer is the work of the Holy Spirit working out the event of rebirth. It is the power of the Holy Spirit working out the redemption of Jesus Christ that ultimately brings new spiritual children into the Kingdom of God (see John 3:3-8). We might refer to this event as conversion. The Holy Spirit brings us into the Kingdom of God.

After being converted, it is critical that each believer acknowledge and walk in the idea that it is the Holy Spirit who helps us to live and to breathe to the glory of God. The Holy Spirit is the one who empowers our conversion, and it is the Holy Spirit who empowers our daily walks.

Could it be that you have missed the daily focus of the Holy Spirit in your life? Did you really think that the one who brought you into the dance of salvation was not going to stay with you and walk with you all the way? Just as He empowered your conversion, the Holy Spirit makes it possible for your daily spiritual success. Be like Elihu – NOT IN A SELF-RIGHTEOUS ATTITUDE – but in his idea of who the Spirit of God is – "The Spirit of God has made me, and the breath of the Almighty gives me life."

FINAL THOUGHT: Take time at the beginning of each day to set your mind on the Holy Spirit's working in your life. Ask Him to fill you each day. Throughout the day, turn your mind and heart to the fact that the Holy Spirit is walking in and with you. Acknowledge in your mind regularly that it is the Holy Spirit enabling and allowing you to have any spiritual success at all.

DAY 4: Will You Become Another Man?
1Samuel 10:6
"Then the Spirit of the LORD will rush upon you, and you will prophesy with them and be turned into another man."

Saul was just beginning his new journey. He had previously been the kid who was simply taller and more athletic than everyone in his grade. He probably was chosen first for the pick games, and girls noticed his big, strong muscles. He kind of had it all going for him.

And then...things changed for Saul. He would no longer be the kid who simply beat everyone in sports, but he was becoming something entirely different. He would be the king over the entire nation. He would no longer be that boy which the guys wanted on their team and the girls wanted on their arms. He was about to be the most powerful and influential man in Israel. He would become the King, and for this to happen the Holy Spirit would come in and make him another man.

In 2008 – 2013 the actor Bryan Cranston played one of the most well-known characters on cable television – and one of the most well-known in history. Cranston played the character Walter White on the series Breaking Bad. It was about a high school chemistry teacher gone bad, and in the show, he becomes one of the largest methamphetamine dealers in the country. Cranston's character became a liar, murderer, thief and drug kingpin. Yet, everyone around Cranston acknowledged that they could never imagine this soft spoken, kindhearted person acting like the character Walter White.

In other words, to play the character on television Bryan Cranston had to somehow become another man. Cranston literally had to become another man in order to play the part of Walter White. This is not uncommon for actors.

In everyday life, there are times when people are changed into brand new people. According to God's Word, every time a person is born again, he or she becomes a brand-new creature (2Cor 5:17). And, in the same way, for a person to live out the life of a brand-new man or woman, it requires the Holy Spirit's work in his or her life. If you are going to live like the new person God made at conversion, then the same Holy Spirit who changed you will be the one continuing to change you.

There are people I have known who could be defined as selfish or arrogant. Years later, I have seen them – knowing that they have become born-again believers – and they are no longer arrogant but are now kind, gentle, selfless and giving. In each case like this, I know that the Holy Spirit turned (them) into another man, just as he did Saul.

FINAL THOUGHT: Acknowledge and recognize in your mind each day that the only way you can be the new creature God made is by the power of the Holy Spirit. God will make a new person out of you, and He will do it through the person of the Holy Spirit. Set your mind daily on the desperate need you have for depending on the Holy Spirit for true change.

DAY 5: The Spirit-Filled Daily Calling
Exodus 31:1-5
"The LORD said to Moses, 'See, I have called by name Bezalel the son of Uri, son of Hur, of the tribe of Judah, and I have filled him with the Spirit of God, with ability and intelligence, with knowledge and all craftsmanship, to devise artistic designs, to work in gold, silver, and bronze, in cutting stones for setting, and in carving wood, to work in every craft.'"

Moses had gone to the mountain to receive the Law of God. From Exodus 24 all the way to Exodus 31, God was relaying His law and commandments to Moses and preparing the tablets that would contain the Law. This Law God was relaying to Moses would be for the future direction and guidance of God's people Israel. Once Moses came down from the mountain with the tablets from God, the Law would be placed before the people to follow.

As God relayed to Moses on the mountain everything from the basic Ten Commandments, to the preparation of Aaron and the priests, to the building of the tabernacle, to feasts which were to be celebrated, He began to finalize His Law. God's preparations for Moses and the Law were so precise that He even laid out His plan for the craftsmen, artisans and carpenters who would build the tabernacle.

God clearly made known that equipping these artisans would be done, not only through their basic abilities, but also through the filling and enabling of the Holy Spirit. Yes…God was filling carpenters, artists and jewel cutters with the power of the Holy Spirit to do their jobs. And you thought God only filled people with His Holy Spirit to do things like preach, pray, witness and teach foreign missions. Think again…

God fills people with His Spirit to do anything and everything that we accomplish for His glory. From preaching, to accounting, to welding, to throwing a baseball, God enables us to do that which we do for His glory.

In the critically acclaimed movie Chariots of Fire, the life and ministry of Eric Liddle is examined. Liddell won a gold and bronze medal in the 1924 Olympics in the 200 and 400 meters, though the 100 meters was his best race. Since the 100-meter qualifying heat was run on Sunday, as a devout Christian missionary, he determined not to run that day. Liddell would later spend his life as a missionary in China until he died at the age of 43 in a Communist internment camp.

One scene in the movie shows a debate with his sister who felt that, at that time, Liddell was more focused on his running than on reaching people. He explained, "God has called me for a purpose, but He has also made me fast. And, when I run, I feel His pleasure!"

Liddell knew what God was explaining to Moses in Exodus 31, and that is that He will fill and enable His people to fulfill those abilities which He has given us. Though God does fill us with His Spirit to preach, sing, witness and teach the Bible, He also fills and empowers us to do carpentry, engineering, music, business management, compete in athletics, accounting, coaching, secretarial, truck driving, practicing law, graphic design and so many more things.

What skills and abilities has God given you? Whatever they are, may you allow Him to fill you with His Spirit that those skills might be used for His great glory.

FINAL THOUGHT: Have you been looking at other believers and thinking "I wish I could _____ (fill in the blank with sing, preach, teach, etc....) like him/her?" Have you considered how God might fill and use you in the very skills you use in school or at work every day to glorify Himself? Begin asking Him to fill you and use you for His glory in your everyday skills.

The Perfect Counselor Study Guide: Week 1

1. Explain how Genesis 1:1-2 describes the Holy Spirit (Spirit of God) before all of the universe was created.

2. What does this statement about the "Spirit of God" in Genesis 1:2 suggest about the existence of God's spirit?

3. As Pharaoh, in Genesis 41:14-36, learned the meaning of his dreams from Joseph, he began looking for a man to prepare the nation for the years of plenty and of famine. In Genesis 41:38, what was the primary qualification this man must possess?

4. Looking back into Genesis 41:14-36, given that Joseph never specifically described the Holy Spirit, where would Pharaoh have known of God's Spirit (i.e. the Holy Spirit) and what that looked like?

5. While Elihu did not comfort Job, he did speak with accurate doctrine. According to Job 33:4, Elihu knew quite well about his origins. He explained that the Holy Spirit did what two things for him?

6. Since Elihu mentions two distinct actions by the Holy Spirit, explain to the best of your knowledge of this passage what the difference is between "God has made me" and "gives me life."

7. Read through 1Samuel 9:27-10:6. Samuel is speaking to the future King Saul in 1Samuel 9:27-10:6. According to 10:6, what power will come upon Saul, and how does Samuel describe the coming of this power?

8. What effect does Samuel say that this power will have on Samuel? Is this something New Testament Christians can relate to? If so, why? (Give a biblical example.)

9. Read through Exodus 31:1-5.

   a. How does God say He will enable Bezalel?

   b. What skills will Bezalel have as a result of this enabling power?

   c. Are these skills what we would normally consider a "call to ministry" in the local church? Why or why not?

DAY 1: No God = No Real Self Control
1Corinthians 3:16a
"Do you not know that you are God's temple…"

In the city of Corinth, in all of its splendor, the great temple of Aphrodite sat atop Mt Acrocorinth as a symbol of paganism, hedonism and sexual immorality. Over 1,000 temple prostitutes "served" the cult of Aphrodite and plied their trade down in the town during the Corinthian nights.

In Corinth, the temple was the symbol of paganism before all of the people. They would have all known of the power and presence of the temple. As Paul exhorts his followers, he utilizes their knowledge of the Temple of Aphrodite. In this case, as he references the temple, he would not have been speaking of the Jerusalem temple, but of the one so prominent and so hedonistic as Aphrodite.

Irony is used to give the Corinthian believers a picture. The picture these believers receive is one of inhabitation – but not of licentious expressions – but of the power of God. Though their image of the inhabitation of the temple might have been immorality and paganism, Paul used that understanding to emphasize the inhabitation and ownership God has in temples – that is the people of God.

In 1Corinthians 3:16, when the Apostle Paul declares in his question "Do you not know that you are God's temple…," he utilizes the second person plural. Literally, he is saying "Do all of you not know that you all are God's temple…" He is speaking of the plurality of believers (i.e. the body of Christ at Corinth). In this particular context Paul is declaring that the local church (each local church) and the overall church is inhabited and owned by God through His Holy Spirit (i.e. the Spirit of Jesus Christ).

Not only does Paul utilize the plural form, but he also uses the possessive form. He wants to emphasize in this declaration (slightly different from 1Corinthians 6:19-20) that the local church is inhabited by God and owned by God.

When we as Christians speak of "our church", we are using a term of affection for the church where we are members and worship, fellowship and serve. And, yet, the reality is that "our church" is not "our church," but it is God's church. The local fellowship of Jesus Christ where a believer is called to worship, learn, fellowship and serve is inhabited, owned and run by Jesus.

It can be a dangerous thing when God's people begin to view the church as if it is their possession. The pastoral leaders, staff, committees, ministries, buildings, programs, music, equipment, property, money and name are all owned by God. God's inhabitation of the local church is a rousing declaration of His ownership of it.

FINAL THOUGHT: Spend some time praising God that He is the resident owner and proprietor of your local church. Spend some time asking to have His complete way in your local church. Ask Him to enable your leadership and staff in a direction according to God's will and plans.

Day 2: Divine Proprietor
1Corinthians 3:16b
"…and that the Spirit of God dwells in you?"

As Paul speaks to the residency of the Holy Spirit (the Spirit of God) in each local church, he does so for the Corinthians in a question form. His question is one that should be easily answered by them, but based on some of their misbehavior, it would appear that they have forgotten. This divine residency in the local church by God is a clear declaration of His possession of it.

The legal journal known as USLegal.com explains it this way:

"Possession means holding property in one's power or the exercise of dominion over property. By having possession, one exercises control over something to the exclusion of all others.

"The saying 'possession is nine points of the law' is an old common law precept that means one who has physical control or possession over the property is clearly at an advantage or is in a better possession than a person who has no possession over the property."

God's residency in the local church, through His Holy Spirit, is a strong manifestation of His ownership and control of that fellowship. As US Legal explains, "Possession means holding property in one's power or the exercise of dominion over property." In the local church, God has established residency through the presence of the Holy Spirit. The Spirit's presence declares possession, possession means ownership and ownership establishes control over what is done. Each local church should be – and must be – directed by the truth of God's Word and the presence of God's Holy Spirit. HE OWNS IT!

My neighbor cannot tell me what color to paint the inside of my house, because I own it. An acquaintance cannot determine what brand of trash bags I should buy, because it is not his money. A co-worker cannot tell me what shoes I should wear today (the brown ones or the black ones...?) because they are my shoes – I own them. Only the owner and possessor determine what happens with a particular entity.

> Only the Owner and Possessor of the local church gets to decide how that fellowship operates. Only the Possessor of the local church should determine what is taught. Only the Possessor of the local church should determine the music that is played. Only the Possessor of the local church should determine the programming that is done. Praise God that we have an owner and resident proprietor in the local church. His ways are always perfect!

FINAL THOUGHT: Spend some time asking God to help you know where you should serve in the local church so that you fulfill His directions for you in your fellowship.

DAY 3: We Must Protect this House!

1Corinthians 3:17a
"If anyone destroys God's temple, God will destroy him."

      The first six chapters of 1Corinthians are mostly filled with Paul addressing, correcting and rebuking the Corinthian church for its problems, including sexual immorality, division, infighting, legal suits and drunkenness (during the Lord's Supper!). The church at Corinth was the church that no one would join, and yet God still desired to see it straightened out and used.

      In this passage of Scripture, Paul is reminding the Corinthian believers of just how important the local church is to God. The church, for God Almighty, is not a side hobby or afterthought. It is the divine bride that His Son paid for with his life. In fact, the church – and its expression through the local church – is so important that Paul declares that God will destroy those who destroy it (in this case referred to as "God's temple").

      It is not unusual for someone to defend his own home. When someone seeks to damage or destroy a place where we live, we take personal offense to that.

      In June 2017 The Baltimore Sun reported:

      "A Lothian couple was at home when an unidentified man tried to break into their house. Taking up a pistol on hearing the noise, the husband tried to force the man from their home at gunpoint but had to shoot when the man lunged at him. Not dissuaded by a wound to the leg, the burglar again tried to attack the husband, whereupon the husband shot the burglar again, giving him a non-fatal head wound, which ended the incident." It is normal and reasonable for someone to defend an attack on their home. Where we live and reside matters to us very much. God, in His infinite wisdom, has established the church through the death, burial and resurrection of His Son Jesus Christ (see Colossians 1). He then inhabits the church (primarily expressed through the local church) by the person and power of His Holy Spirit. The local church is the "temple" in which Jesus Christ dwells through the Person of the Holy Spirit. Any attack and/or offense against the local church is an offense against God.

Our involvement, worship and ministry in our local church is an expression of our fellowship with our Savior. Our Savior has won our salvation and our place of worship with His very life. Your worship, fellowship, discipleship and service in the local church is far more than simply an activity – it is an expression of love to a Savior who won it for you with his blood. Let's worship, fellowship, grow and serve in our local church with the knowledge that it is a gift from our Savior!

FINAL THOUGHT: Spend some time prayerfully (maybe even making a list in a journal) praising God for the ways in which His "temple" – the local church – has blessed you, your family and your friends. Also, spend some time praying for your local church and maybe 2-3 others in your community to effectively celebrate Christ; connect believers more deeply with Christ and commission believers to go out and win the lost.

DAY 4: The Transfer of Ownership
1Corinthians 6:19
"Or do you not know that your body is a temple of the Holy Spirit within you, whom you have from God? You are not your own."

Having confronted the Corinthians (the church members) on everything from divisions in the church (1Corinthians 1:10-17) to political parties in the fellowship (1Corinthians 3:5-17) to sexual immorality in the fellowship (1Corinthians 5:1-8) to frivolous secular lawsuits between members (1Corinthians 6:1-7), Paul clarifies God's position on these matters. He unequivocally reminds the Corinthians of the kinds of lifestyles that are not part of the lives true believers (1Corinthians 6:9-10). Furthermore, the Apostle clearly states that those who live lifestyles like those mentioned in 6:9-10 are not born-again people and will face eternal punishment without Christ.

Paul goes on to explain the position of the Gospel for believers relative to lifestyle choices. In 1Cor. 6:12-14, he helps the believers to understand that, while clear and ongoing sin is an offense to God, the reality is that God allows men and women the opportunity to make clear choices of activities and life choices. And, while many of these life choices are acceptable for us, not all of them are helpful. And…that being the case, the guiding truth and reality for every believer on how to make these critical, day to day lifestyle choices is found in 1Cor. 6:19 in what one might call the "Ownership Principle." If one is not certain of a choice related to some area or activity, ask the owner what he thinks.

In this case, when a believer turns himself/herself over to Christ and is saved, he also is turning ownership over to the new resident – the Holy Spirit (who is God). Once I was saved, I was giving full rights of ownership over to God and His resident person – the Holy Spirit.

Once, my bride and I sold a house that we owned. After we finished the closing at the attorney's office, we left and drove to our new home. After some days, I was looking through a drawer at home and came across some old keys. I realized immediately that one of those keys was to the house we had just sold.

That means that I still had a key that, just days before, would have lawfully allowed me to unlock the doors to a house that was now unlawful for me to enter without permission. What was the difference between that key and the same key just days before? The difference was the transfer of ownership. We had transferred ownership of that house to someone who had rightfully purchased it. That house was no longer ours to come and go as we like!

At the moment of conversion (justification) each believer is forgiven, prepared a seat in heaven (Ephesians 2:1-8) and surrenders bodily ownership to God. Proof of this new ownership by God is the new resident, and that is the person of the Holy Spirit. One of the best things you can possibly do as a follower of Jesus Christ is to be certain you have fully yielded all ownership activities of your life, mind, will and body to God.

FINAL THOUGHT: Take some moments to prayerfully offer praise and adoration to Christ for taking ownership of your life. Also, take some time to prayerfully ask God to show you by the Holy Spirit if there are attitudes, actions, words or thoughts that are not yet under His full ownership.

DAY 5: A High Price
1Corinthians 6:20
"…for you were bought with a price. So glorify God in your body."

Paul underscores for Christians that sexual sin is a special offense because it is against Christ and against these bodies for which Christ paid dearly. In fact, in addition to reminding us as believers that the Holy Spirit indwells each believer (6:19), he also points out the fact that these bodies were purchased at a high price.

It is now, and has always been, important to know how valuable something is – or how much of a price was paid for it. In fact, the more expensive an item is then the more care we generally take of it.

When my dear bride and I were first married, we moved into a little one-bedroom apartment. It had one bathroom. She proceeded to set up our house and hung some towels in the bathroom on the towel racks. Shortly after I washed my hands and dried them, then I went about my way.

A few minutes later, my bride called out to me with some urgency. I went to her standing outside the bathroom (which, because of the small size of the apartment was essentially outside kitchen and in front of the front door and the entrance to the bedroom…). She proceeded to passionately explain to me why these expensive towels were not to be used to dry our hands, but that they were special towels. They were meant to be decorative.

Though the expensive towels did a fine job of drying my hands, they were to be carefully displayed and not used for something so common as hand drying. We had older, less expensive towels to be used for the hand drying job.

Expensive towels get treated better than cheap ones. And so most anything else.

Paper plates get thrown away, while expensive china is displayed carefully and used only occasionally.

A $2,000.00 automobile is going to be treated differently than a $102,000.00 automobile.

A stainless-steel chain purchased from a retail store is going to be treated quite differently than a solid gold necklace purchased from an expensive jewelry store.

No matter what is being discussed, the more expensive the item then the more valuable it is considered.

Romans 5:8 explains, "…but God shows His love for us in that while we were still sinners, Christ died for us," The cost of purchasing us was the life of the Beloved of God, the Second Person of the Trinity and the Son of Man. The greatest price was paid for me, and so the value of these bodies is immense.

Treating our bodies haphazardly is poorly treating an enormously valuable purchase. As a child of God, I must do that which is most pleasing to the one who spent so much to purchase me…my Savior Jesus Christ.

FINAL THOUGHT: Is there any, activity, action, attitude or behavior in your life that is simply not worthy of the price Jesus Christ paid for you? Spend some time laying it specifically and honestly before the Lord and asking Him to help you move forward in a way that reflects the price paid for you.

The Perfect Counselor Study Guide: Week 2

1. In 1Corinthians 3:16, Paul is speaking to the church body. Because he utilizes the second person plural of "you", then we know he is speaking to the whole fellowship and not just an individual believer. He asks a rhetorical question of the church. What is that question?

2. Why would it be important for a local church fellowship to "know" that they are God's temple? (See Ephesians 1:22-23; Colossians 1:17-18 for more insight.)

3. In 1Corinthians 3:16, as Paul speaks to the church, He declares that "the Spirit of God" dwells in the church. Read Galatians 5:22-23 that speaks to individual believers who are indwelt by the Holy Spirit. Write down a list of characteristics from Galatians 5:22-23 and, for each characteristic, how that might look in the individual believer's life.

4. If 1Corinthians 3:16b is speaking to the church body indwelt by the Holy Spirit and Galatians 5:22-23 is speaking to how it looks when individual believers are controlled by the Spirit, describe some specific characteristics the local church will display.

5. Paul lays out a dangerous condition in 3:17 and the consequence of that condition. Read the following passages and explain why they are relevant to 1Corinthians 3:17.

   a. Acts 5:1-11

   b. Galatians 1:6-10

6. In 1Corinthians 6:19 Paul speaks in terms that sound quite similar to 3:17, and yet 6:19 is speaking in the singular form. This means that

"Or do you not know" is referring to individual Christians. Why is this quite different, and yet similar, to 1Corinthians 3:17?

7. The final declaration in 1Corinthians 6:19 is regarding the ownership of these "earth suits" (as author Bill Gilliam used to call them). What does Paul say about their ownership, and why does that matter in our day to day lives?

8. What does 1Corinthians 6:20 have to say regarding how the ownership of these bodies came to be?

9. The conclusion of NOT owning our own bodies, is a declaration to end this verse in 1Corinthians 6:20. The word "glorify" comes from the Greek do-za, which literally means "to express one's opinion of." Write this verse out with the statement "express the opinion of" in place of "glorify."

EXTRA THOUGHTS

Martin Luther (the great reformer) once said, "I have held many things in my hand, and have lost them all; but whatever I have placed in God's hands that I still possess."

No God = No True Self Control.

God's Ownership = True Self Control

The Holy Spirit resides in every single Christian and verifies ownership of that life, that body and that person. When you claim Christ as Lord of your life, you also declare Him as having ownership over your very body and activities, words, ideas and actions. Only He – as the owner – has the right to determine what I do each moment.

Take some time today to declare God's ownership of your life. Ask the Holy Spirit to give you the victory and power to have your life – and your body – reflect His wishes in what you say, what you do and how you act.

DAY 1: Hey Mom…Would You Ask Dad for Me…?
John 14:6
"And I will ask the Father, and he will give you another Helper, to be with you forever,"

As John 14 begins, Jesus is explaining to his disciples of his need to leave and go away. And, while Jesus' leaving makes perfect sense to modern day followers of Christ (2,000 years in hindsight), it was confusing, disturbing and scary for Jesus' disciples at that time. As he began his explanation of his departure, Jesus had to urge the disciples not to have troubled hearts (which is why we believe that they must have had troubled hearts…).

In order to help his most loyal and trusted followers have peace in their hearts, Jesus explains the help he will provide while he is gone. In explaining and describing this help, Jesus assures them that this help will come as a result of him asking "…the Father…" Not only would the disciples be assured of a Helper coming to them, but Jesus lets them know that he will ask the Father himself for this Helper. The disciples needed not be concerned at an answer to their need, because Jesus would ask the Father on their behalf. Whew…! That must have been a relief.

When my kids were little, they learned some key truths about relating to mom and dad. Thankfully, my youngest child has been at a big advantage, as she learned some of these keys from her two older siblings.

My eldest once told my youngest this wise truth, "Sarah Elisabeth, when dad makes up his mind on something, arguing with him or begging is not going to change his mind. There is only one person who can change dad's mind, and that is mom. If you want to get dad to decide, or change his mind on something, you better get mom to do that for you."

It sure is nice to have someone speak to the head person on your behalf. When I know I have an extremely qualified person petitioning the head person on my behalf, it does several things for me. One, it assures me that my request will be heard clearly. Two, it assures me that my request will be responded to with authority. Three, it assures me that the "head person's" answer will be helpful.

32

Jesus Christ is our Savior and Lord. He has petitioned the Father on our behalf, and the Holy Spirit is our personal answer in these days. In other words, as a born-again child of God, you can know that the entire Trinity is at work on your behalf to help you walk through this day...and every day. Remember, Jesus has already asked the Father!

Final Thought: Ask God to help you rest in the idea that the Father has you. Jesus is petitioning Him for EVERYTHING you need, and the Holy Spirit is personally walking you through this life as your Counselor, Comforter and Guide.

DAY 2: Lifetime Warranty
John 14:16
"And I will ask the Father, and he will give you another Helper, to be with you forever…"

As Jesus described His going away – the crucifixion, resurrection and ascension to the Father – He was also sure to explain to his disciples how he would provide for them while he was gone. These men, who had been walking daily with Christ for three years, were at a loss to understand what they would do without their Rabbi and teacher.

Jesus explained that, while he was gone, he would provide another Helper. This word Helper (Comforter, Counselor) is the Greek word paraclete. It is para, which means "beside" and kaleo, which means "called." This Comforter and Counselor was one who was "called along beside." In other words, Jesus was explaining to his disciples that, while he was gone to the Father, he would send another specifically to be "called alongside them."

What a relief it was to those men to know that one with the same power and presence would come alongside them, even as Christ was gone from them. And, not only was this Helper coming alongside these disciples, but Jesus also explained that He would be with them "…forever…" It is one thing to know that I have help and support, but it is another thing entirely to know that I have it forever.

My bride and I are in our third year driving our crossover SUV. We purchased it new, and it has been extremely helpful and comforting knowing that anything malfunctioning on it was covered by a warrantee. The car manufacturer came alongside us and agreed to be of help whenever we need it…up to a certain mileage. That help which the car manufacturer provides is help for a limited amount of time. And, while it has been quite nice knowing that we have this help, we also know that the help will end, and we will be on our own to repair or replace anything that might malfunction.

As followers of Jesus Christ, God has not sent us a Helper and Comforter to come alongside for a limited time. He has sent every true born-again child of God a Helper and Comforter to come alongside and help with our daily walk…FOREVER.

I never need worry about the warrantee on our Helper running out, because He is eternally with us.

We never need worry about our Helper quitting on us because He is eternally beside us.

We never need worry about this Counselor leaving us because He is infinitely there for us.

We never need to worry about this Counselor being stumped by our problem because He is infinitely wise.

Take heart for every born-again child of God...the Holy Spirit is your forever Counselor and Comforter.

FINAL THOUGHT: Spend some time in worship and praise to God for your forever Helper and Comforter. Consider using some songs of worship during this time that sing of the power and presence of the Holy Spirit in your life!

DAY 3: Jimmy Lunchbox and the Controlling Power of the Holy Spirit
John 14:17
"even the Spirit of truth, whom the world cannot receive, because it neither sees him nor knows him. You know him, for he dwells with you and will be in you. As Jesus continued his explanation to his disciples of the plan in place for him leaving, he represented the one coming (the Helper and Counselor) as "the Spirit of truth." In other words, as he leaves and sends someone back in his place, this someone would be guaranteed to provide truth and clarity to the followers of Christ.

For the previous three years, the disciples learned the things to trust – and not trust – by the audible words of Jesus to them. However, if their teacher and rabbi left to go away, how would they know what was true, real and genuine…if their Truth Teller was gone away? Jesus explained that a new person would come to them on his behalf, and that this person would not only speak truth, but He would give them the very spirit of truth.

It is one thing for someone to tell me what is true and what is not true. It is another thing entirely for that someone to speak truth through me, so that I am not hearing through my ears but through my mind and soul.

In the comedy movie Old Dogs, Dan (played by Robin Williams) is having trouble relating to his young daughter. She wants him to play tea party, but he doesn't know what to do. His best friend Charlie (John Travolta) decides to hire Jimmy Lunchbox (Bernie Mac) to help. Jimmy Lunchbox gives Dan a suit to wear that will be controlled by a remote that Charlie holds in another room. As Dan sits down to play tea party with his daughter, Charlie controls his moves and words from a remote control in another room.

Dan seems to be winning his daughter's affection as he is controlled by this suit. In fact, everything was working out good until water gets spilled on the suit and it short circuits!

Dan, Charlie and Jimmy Lunchbox figured out what many believers need to learn. When a person has an outside source controlling them, it is hard to go wrong.

Christ promised his disciples that he would send back the Spirit of Truth when he went away. That promise is still true for every single follower of Christ. Christians do not just have someone telling them truth, but we have someone dwelling within us who, if we allow Him, will speak truth through us and direct us to all truth.

God wants you to know His Truth so much that, if you are a born-again believer, He has sent the Holy Spirit to dwell within you and speak truth to and through you. Every Christian has inside of him or her the Spirit of Truth, which means that the Holy Spirit in us is filled with and expresses the truth of God.

PRAISE GOD THAT HIS VERY MIND OF TRUTH IS DWELLING IN YOU AS A CHILD OF GOD!

FINAL THOUGHT: Spend some time meditating on Proverbs 1:1-7. As you do, jot down special ideas or thoughts the Holy Spirit – The Spirit of Truth - gives to you as you read.

DAY 4: It's Not my Daddy's Glasses
John 14:17
"…even the Spirit of truth, whom the world cannot receive, because it neither sees him nor knows him. You know him, for he dwells with you and will be in you."

As Jesus describes and defines the One who will come be with His followers, as He descends to heaven – and before He returns – He refers to the one as "the Spirit of Truth." Jesus, of course is talking of the Holy Spirit. The Holy Spirit is the third person of the Trinity, and He is a person who has been sent to every believer as the very life and power of Christ to enable and walk with us.

Not only does Jesus describe the Holy Spirit by calling him Spirit of Truth, but He contrasts the Spirit with the understanding of the world. In fact, Jesus clearly explains that the Holy Spirit in us will not be received by the world – in fact, He cannot be seen by the world. Jesus explains that, though the Holy Spirit is the One whom enables us to know and truth (Spirit of Truth) clearly, He is just as unclear to this world system.

As sharply focused as truth is to Christians with the Holy Spirit in us, it is just that blurry and unclear to the world. Believers have Spirit-filled, spiritual lenses through which to see truth clearly. The world does not have this prescription filled by Dr. Holy Spirit, so looking through the lens of the Holy Spirit for the world simply makes things blurry.

When I was a little boy, I was never required to wear glasses. My eyesight was sharp, and I never had a need for prescription glasses, contacts or any eyesight assistance. My father was required to wear glasses that were a strong prescription. He could see fine with his glasses, but without them the world was blurry and unclear. In all honesty, without his glasses, he was unable to see the most basic things. With his prescription glasses on, his sight was clear.

One day, I decided that I thought it was cool to wear glasses. My dad had a pair of back up glasses on his nightstand, so one day I tried them on. As soon as they went on my face, I realized something was horribly wrong! The glasses that made my dad's sight clear were the same ones that now made the whole world look like sludge to me. Those glasses that were so effective for him were completely ineffective for me. Those glasses were his prescription and not mine, so what made things clear for him made them blurry and unintelligible for me.

When we are born again, the Holy Spirit of God comes to live in us. He is precisely the prescription that every Christian needs to see God's truth, justice, love, holiness, compassion and grace clearly. Yet, the same Holy Spirit, who is the prescription for spiritual eyes, is blurry and distorted for those without Christ. No true believer should ever think that the world is going to see biblical truth and God's design clearly like us, because the Spirit of Truth is only the correct prescription for God's children.

Believer, you have the Holy Spirit – the Spirit of Truth – and it is Him alone who enables you to see God's world with clarity. This world system cannot see God's plans clearly because they do not have the capacity for the prescription of the Spirit of Truth

FINAL THOUGHT: Think of people around you who are unsaved, and with whom you possibly have a major difference of opinion. Begin calling on God to save them, and do not become frustrated with the difference. After all, your prescription (the Spirit of Truth) will not work for them. Ask God to change their prescription!

DAY 5: Speaking Through Me
John 14:17
"…even the Spirit of truth, whom the world cannot receive, because it neither sees him nor knows him. You know him, for he dwells with you and will be in you."

It is hard to imagine the disciples attempting to absorb the teachings of Christ at this point. They are already disheartened with the idea that Christ is leaving and going away. Jesus is instructing them to let them know that there will be one coming for them in His place. Jesus is explaining to his disciples that it is better that He leaves, so that the Spirit of Truth can come walk with them.

Then…this bombshell! You know him, for he dwells with you and will be IN YOU (italics and bold added by me…). How can they decipher the idea of the one to come living IN them? It would not be that difficult understanding God's Spirit to guide them, but how were they to absorb this concept of that same Holy Spirit living on the inside?

It is one thing to know that this teacher, rabbi, friend and guide was going away and would send someone back in his place (not that they completely understood yet where Christ was going), but to conceive of this same one living in them was an entirely different concept. Could any of us have reasoned through the idea of this one who was talking to us ultimately sending back a powerful person who would talk to us – and in us? Someone who speaks to us from outside our person is understandable, but how does one absorb the idea of this Spirit of Truth speaking to us inside our person and through our very own minds?

Imagine a movie scene (played out in any number of movies) where the brutish, unromantic and uninspiring guy attempts to win the beautiful girl. He has no skills to talk with her or say the correct thing, but his friend – who is poetic and romantic – concocts a plan. The brutish friend will put a small, wireless earpiece in his ear. The romantic friend will be at the other end of this connection with some sort of two-way device that allows him to hear the conversation and speak to his romantically inept friend.

The unskilled guy somehow finds a way to set up a time to meet with his potential lady. As he meets with her, the friend on the other end speaks to him and passes along to him all the correct things to say. You see, the romantic friend is not just standing by speaking the words to his inept friend, but he is essentially speaking these words through the ear of his friend.

God, in His plan of redemption, determined that, not only did we need Him speaking to us from the outside source (the Bible, preaching, teaching, etc...), but His children need Him speaking through us. In fact, Jesus once even told his disciples that, when they went to preach the Gospel, there would be times where they would be persecuted and arrested. In those particular times, they need not worry about what to say but that God would speak through them.

Every single day, born again believers get out of bed knowing that we have a God who speaks to us and speaks through us. The Spirit of Truth lives within every believer, so that we are enabled – as we listen to Him – to understand and speak God's mind in our everyday lives.

FINAL THOUGHT: Take your time and read through this text slowly and repeatedly: Ezekiel 36:27. As you read and meditate, jot down thoughts, ideas and application God is showing you.

The Perfect Counselor Study Guide: Week 3

1. In John 14:16 Jesus explains what He will ask the Father. This is God the Son letting his disciples know that He planned to speak to God the Father on their behalf. Read Hebrews 7:23-25. What role does Christ play in speaking to God on our behalf?

2. Jesus was telling His disciples that, while he was going away (had been temporarily with them), He was sending a permanent helper. For them, this meant that they would never have to face this sad goodbye again that they were about to experience when Christ left. Take a look at Deuteronomy 31:6. While the Old Testament saints may not have understood how God could fulfill that, how is John 14:16 relevant to that statement?

3. Consider the following verses and how they can relate to John 14:16b "with you forever." Jot down at least one way that each of these verses relate to John 14:16b.

   a. Genesis 28:15
   b. John 10:28
   c. Philippians 1:6
   d. Hebrews 13:5-6

4. What does Jesus call the Holy Spirit at the beginning of John 14:17, and what does that title mean?

5. This Spirit of truth has what relationship to those of this world? Why?

6. This Spirit of truth has what relationship to a true, born-again Christian? Why?

7. For each of these verses or passages below, give a one or two statement reason that they relate to Jesus' statement about the Spirit of Truth in God's people.

    a. Nehemiah 9:20
    b. John 16:4
    c. 1Corinthians 2:9-16
    d. 1John 2:27

THE PERFECT COUNSELOR DEVOTIONS: WEEK 4
Alone with God

DAY 1: Maybe I Should Just Go…
John 16:7
"Nevertheless, I tell you the truth: it is to your advantage that I go away, for if I do not go away, the Helper will not come to you. But if I go, I will send him to you."

The night before Christ was crucified, he gathered with his key friends and disciples. His main twelve disciples still seemed not to understand what was coming. Jesus spent a lot of time preparing these men for his departure, as he explained and expounded on the One he would send back to them on his behalf.

As Jesus attempted to explain his departure, these men reacted before hearing the whole story. It appears that they reacted with grief and hurt, even as Jesus attempted to tell them that he would be going away (John 14:1a; 14:6). At this point, Christ scolded them and explained that, while they may not understand his going, it was better for them than if he stayed.

Too often, understanding the way God is working means knowing that the trial or disappointment we face might do more for us than if it did not happen at all. We must know that God has a plan – just as Christ had a plan for leaving (i.e. sending the Holy Spirit back).

When I was eleven, and about to head to junior high school, my dad came one day and explained that his company was moving him. He was a salesman for a national company, and they were moving his territory to Georgia and Alabama. At that time, we had lived in southern Indiana for six years. I had gone through elementary school there and had developed many close friends. I had established myself in athletics, and coaches at the junior high level knew me.

Moving from there was a shock to me, and it was difficult for me to understand. In fact, it felt as if my entire world was being turned upside down, as I left all of my friends, familiar areas and experiences behind.

We moved to Warner Robins, Georgia, and it took me a while to begin to feel even a bit adjusted – let alone accepting. I look back on that move and realize that it was Warner Robins, Georgia, where I was invited to the church where I would eventually confess Christ and be born again. It was Warner Robins, Georgia, where I met the young lady who is now my wife, my best friend and the mother of all three of my children – as well as my ministry partner for life. It was Warner Robins, Georgia, where I first sensed that God was calling me to preach, and where I served one of my first staff positions at a local church.

As it turned out, the move my dad made – purely as a part of his job – was one of the best things that happened to me. In the grand scheme of things, what I thought was possibly ruining my life was one of the most important things that ever happened to me. Now, I praise God for that move.

As you face life challenges today that seem to be against you, remember Jesus' conversation with his disciples as he went away. The Holy Spirit coming to us was contingent on Jesus leaving. If the disciples would have had their way at that moment, they never would have received the Holy Spirit – and neither would any of us. PRAISE BE TO GOD THAT HE WENT AWAY!

FINAL THOUGHT: Take a few moments and think of one or two of the most challenging events or experiences in your life right now. Spend some time lifting those events up to God and acknowledging that He has a plan for you. Though these experiences are difficult now, praise Him for how He will use them for His glory and your good.

DAY 2: He's Speaking for Me
John 16:8
'And when he comes, he will convict the world concerning sin and righteousness and judgment..."

By this point in John's Gospel, Jesus had spent an extensive amount of time teaching his disciples about His going and the coming of the Holy Spirit. He has established for them that, even though they are distraught that he is going, it is best that he does go. Furthermore, in John 14, Jesus laid out instruction on just how the Holy Spirit would serve as a parent ("I will not leave you as orphans." – John 14:18) and a promise of His return (John 14:3).

In John 15, Jesus explains how the Holy Spirit will work in the lives of believers. He uses the image of a vine, branches and fruit to express how the Holy Spirit will work through believers.

In John 16, Jesus offers a clear picture on how the Holy Spirit will work to enable believers to reach the lost with the Gospel. Once again, in John 16:6, he briefly scolds the disciples for becoming upset that he is leaving without asking him why and where ("But because I have said these things to you, sorrow has filled your heart."). He goes on to explain that, as he goes, it is better for them. Not only that, but as he goes, he shares his plan to send someone back who will speak to the world.

Jesus uses the term "convict the world." He is speaking of how the Holy Spirit will reveal to the world their need for salvation.

CONVICT:

Verb:	declare (someone) to be guilty of a criminal offense
Noun:	a person found guilty of a criminal offense and serving a sentence of imprisonment.

In this statement, Jesus is letting his disciples – and ultimately all Christian disciples today – know that the Holy Spirit will come and do the job of revealing the lost world's lostness to them. The word "convict," throughout the New Testament, is always used in reference to lost people. The Holy Spirit will do the job of showing a lost person that he or she is guilty in relation to sin, lack of righteousness and future judgement.

As Christians, we are called to share the Gospel of Christ in our words (Matthew 28:19-20; 1Peter 3:15) and in our lifestyles (Galatians 5:16,22). We share the message, but it is the Holy Spirit who changes the hearts and minds of those in this world. Do not miss this liberating message!

When we share Christ with the lost, the primary job is to share the message. And, while believers share the message, the Holy Spirit is working in the minds and hearts of those to whom we witness to show them their need. Nothing you or I do will bring conviction on the lost person. Only the Holy Spirit can do this! So…good news child of God! Share Christ in your words and in your lifestyle – knowing that, as you do that, the Comforter is working in the mind and hearts of the lost to make them open and available for the message! HE IS WORKING ON YOUR BEHALF!!

FINAL THOUGHT: Ask God to help you prepare to clearly share the Gospel with the lost and praise Him for going ahead of you to open the hearts and minds of the lost to be available to the message.

DAY 3: They Don't Know What They Don't Know
John 16:8
"And when he comes, he will convict the world concerning sin and righteousness and judgment…"

In helping the disciples understand His need to go away, Jesus explained the benefit and help that would come if He left+. In His absence, He explained (John 16:7) the Holy Spirit would come to them.

Part of Christ's master plan of redemption was to ascend to the Father, while sending back the Holy Spirit to do great works worldwide. As the Holy Spirit was to be sent to do these works on earth in Christ's absence, Jesus explained in more specific detail one of the ways in which He would work on earth.

Jesus declared, "he will convict the world concerning sin." The Holy Spirit was being sent to earth, in part, to cause lost people to become aware of their sin. In becoming aware of the sin in their lives, it would be at this point that the unsaved would see the need to be forgiven and saved. Without knowing one is lost, why would one want to be found? Without knowing one has committed sin, why would one want forgiveness of sin? Without a person knowing he has been separated, he will never desire to be reconnected.

A lost person without any real knowledge or understanding of why he or she needs to be saved is a little like the lost pilot of the commercial airliner. He came over the P.A. system and announced,

"Ladies and gentlemen, this is your pilot speaking. I hope you are having a pleasant flight. "I have some news to share with you. Part of it is bad and part of it is good. The bad news is that we are completely lost and really do not know where we are or where we are headed.
"The good news is that we are making great time."

An airplane needs a pilot who understands how bad it is to be lost. And, an unsaved person, if he or she is to ever be born again, must come to an awareness of his lostness. How does this happen? How does a person who is completely lost become aware of his spiritual state?

Certainly, Christians are to carry the Gospel to those who are lost, but what happens if the people to whom we carry it are not interested in the message or aware of their need? According to the words of Christ, it is the Holy Spirit who will make a lost person aware of his or her sin.

Our job is to be faithful in delivering the message. The Holy Spirit, on this earth, will work in the heart and mind of the lost person to help him or her see their lostness and sin.

This is a great word of liberation to every believer. We are free from producing results as believers. Our only requirement is to be out sharing the message. Only the Holy Spirit can cause someone to see he or she is caught in sin. Only the Holy Spirit can cause a lost person to see that he or she is lost and in need of being found.

Child of God, as you go, be ready to give an answer. Be ready to share. Be ready to tell others of Christ. But...know that only the Holy Spirit can ultimately make a person listen or take notice.

FINAL THOUGHT: Take some time to think about opportunities you may have in the coming days to share the Gospel. What is going to be your best opportunity – verbally, a written Gospel tract, a text message, an email or a card or letter. Pray asking God to prepare the hearts of those with whom you will share.

DAY 4: Virtual Reality
John 16:10
"…concerning righteousness, because I go to the Father, and you will see me no more…"

Jesus continued his teaching to his disciples regarding his going away. He explained that, once he left, He would send the Holy Spirit back. This Holy Spirit would dwell in people and would work in the hearts of those who were lost. One of the areas of conviction the Holy Spirit would bring to the lost would be regarding righteousness.

While Christ walked on earth, people could look at him and see righteousness incarnate. The words Jesus spoke were righteous. The attitudes Jesus displayed were perfectly righteous. The actions Jesus carried out were perfectly righteous. In every way, Jesus Himself was righteousness for all the world to see…and to realize how far short they fall. Upon realizing this shortcoming, lost people would again look to Christ for help.

However, once Christ was crucified, buried, resurrected and ascended to heaven, people would not be able to see righteousness…unless there were another way. This other way of observing righteousness was the Holy Spirit coming and working through Christians – and in the hearts of the lost world – to bring conviction on them of just exactly what righteousness looked like. The Holy Spirit would show lost people what Jesus incarnate had shown them before he left the earth – what righteousness looked like compared to human "righteousness."

In today's culture, the term VR has become big business and creates an enormous base of clientele. Those letters stand for Virtual Reality. This technology produces images and video type experiences that simulate real life. Virtual Reality can be simulated experiences for athletics, driving, flying, fighting and other experiences.

The images in a VR experience look like the people they represent, but they are not actually the people they represent. The VR characters attempt to be an exact representation of the buildings, animals, vehicles, children, adolescents or scenes they emulate.

The VR technology has become wildly popular because people love the idea of experiencing certain things while never having to leave their Lay-Z-Boy chair. These VR experiences give us the exact representation of the things we seek. An unathletic person can become a real NBA, NFL or MLB star with VR technology. A fan of a celebrity can meet that person in a way that seems like real life. A military member can practice shooting, flying or even fighting with VR technology and it seems real. This technology to create a virtual reality experience can only simulate something in place of the real thing. And yet, people flock to it by the millions.

Christ, in all of His wisdom, sent back the Holy Spirit to earth that He might live through every born-again believer. As he lives through us, His righteousness is seen through our words, actions and attitudes. In other words, the righteousness of Jesus Christ – which was seen in Him as He walked bodily on earth – is now seen as He replicates His life through believers on earth. This is now the only way a lost person can truly see the righteousness that he or she needs to begin to desire to be born again. And...this is accomplished through the VR component of the Godhead – the Holy Spirit.

If you allow the Holy Spirit to live through your life, then the unsaved around you have the opportunity to see righteousness and be drawn to it.

FINAL THOUGHT: Read Galatians 5:16-26. List some of the expressions of righteousness that will come out of your life if the Holy Spirit is living the life of Christ through you. As you do, remember that these are not your behaviors, but they are the expression of God Himself through you.

DAY 5: Did You Wash Your Hands?
John 16:11
"...concerning judgment, because the ruler of this world stands judged..."

As Jesus explained the areas in which the Holy Spirit would enable believers to speak to the lost world, one of the areas that He discussed was judgement. He explained to his disciples that one of the areas of conviction in the hearts of the lost would be judgement.

Christ was making application to his earlier comments in John 16:10, when he said that the Holy Spirit would "convict the world regarding...judgement...".   Conviction regarding judgement would be necessary because no one wants to face the fact that he or she will be held accountable for their sin. And, when one is held accountable for unforgiven sin, it requires judgement.

Judgement means penalty.   Judgement means accountability. Judgement means fear. Judgement means punishment. Judgement means exposure. Not many want to think about judgement, and yet one must face it if he or she is to come to terms with their need for Christ – and the forgiveness He offers.

How can a Christian go about sharing the Gospel and convincing an unbeliever to realize that he is facing judgement? After all, once I tell someone that he is facing eternal judgement – alongside the "ruler of this world" (aka Satan) – he might not listen to me anymore. Is there a way to convince him of this impending judgement? Jesus explains in this verse that it is the Holy Spirit who performs that kind of convicting power. If a person comes to realize his future is with judgement and Satan, and he or she repents at this realization, then it was not a person who showed him but the Holy Spirit who. It is as if the Holy Spirit reveals things to a lost person that simply cannot be seen by human eyes.

When I was a little boy in school, one of the things we were taught and encouraged to do was to wash our hands. We were told that, when we play, touch other things, use the bathroom or handle dirt, small bugs (referred to as germs) crawl all over our hands waiting to make us sick.

In fact, I was told that these germs are so small that the human eye cannot see them. They are so small that not even a regular magnifying glass can see these germs. In order for a person to see these germs, it takes a very special piece of equipment called a microscope. And, even under a microscope, the average person would have no idea of the potential danger of these germs.

Doctors, scientists and research scientists had long ago discovered these germs and determined that they could be quite harmful to people. As a small child, the only reason I knew about or believed in these dangerous germs was because someone with insight, wisdom, knowledge and clear vision saw them and shared it with me. I was shown blown-up pictures in my textbooks of these awful germs. I was told in books by these brilliant men that I needed to be concerned about these germs, and so I needed to wash my hands. It was their insight that compelled me to act and no one else.

In the same way that scientists helped convince me of the danger of germs that I simply would never have seen, the Holy Spirit convinces lost people of the danger of judgement hanging over them. As a believer, it is your calling to carry the message of Jesus and his salvation to the lost. It is your calling to explain salvation, but it is not your job to convince lost people of their lostness or future judgement. While you should explain it, know that the only way a lost person is open to hearing about judgement is when the Holy Spirit opens his or her heart.

FINAL THOUGHT: Think about an unsaved person – or people – who you may know who wants to hear nothing about judgement – and even may be hostile to it. Pray for them that the Holy Spirit will open their hearts.

The Perfect Counselor Study Guide: Week 4

1. In John 16:7, Jesus explained to His disciples something that they had trouble digesting. He was trying to let them know that it was better for Him to go than stay. At times, God does things that seem worse rather than better to us, and yet these things are actually better rather than worse. Take a look at these other instances of God doing worse to make it better for His people, and then write down a memory of something where that has happened to you – you thought it was worse, but really it was God doing better for you.

     a. Genesis 50:15-21
     b. Acts 7:54-8:1, 4

2. In John 16:7 Jesus explained that He would send The Helper (Counselor). Read Acts 2:1-13. How did this event in Acts fit with John 16:7?

3. Jesus explains in John 16:8-11 what kind of ministry the Holy Spirit will have in helping believers to reach the lost "world." Jesus explains that the Holy Spirit will "convict." This word is especially speaking of the work that the Holy Spirit does in the mind and soul of lost people. In fact, this word convict is never used in the New Testament relative to believers, since born-again believers are no longer CON-victs (noun) to sin. Neither are believers con-VICTED (verb) as being guilty.
    Consider these questions below.

     a. According to John 16:8, what will be the three areas of conviction brought on by the Holy Spirit to the world?

     b. After reading John 16:9, why does the Holy Spirit need to convict lost people of sin? (Answer in your own words....)

    c. Next, in John 16:10 Jesus explains that the Holy Spirit will convict the world of righteousness. What specific reason does He give for that area of conviction? (again…write this in your own words to be sure you understand it.)

    d. Finally, in John 16:11 Jesus finishes by pointing out the convicting of righteousness. Why would this be necessary?

4. Consider John 16:8-11 and the convicting power the Holy Spirit is going to do in the hearts and minds of the lost people to whom we witness. Knowing that HE and HE ALONE will do that convicting, what is the job of each believer in alerting the lost world of their need?

DAY 1: The Trinity at Work on My Behalf
John 15:1
"I am the true vine, and my Father is the vinedresser."

As Jesus explained to his disciples in John 14 that he was leaving in order that he might send back the Holy Spirit to them, he continues the message in John 15. In this chapter, Jesus explains the way in which the Holy Spirit will work through his followers once he is gone.

The images Christ uses to explain the working of the Holy Spirit are two parts – a vine (true vine to be exact) and vine dresser. The vine is the main part of the plant. The vine is the main source through which nutrients are channeled and carried to the needed appendages. The vine is what truly makes the plan alive.

The vinedresser – or farmer – oversees the health and work of the vine. The vinedresser works to ensure that the vine and its corresponding plant parts are healthy and in proper place. The farmer works daily to tend that which ensures a healthy vine growth and effective vine production.

The ultimate production of this plant is fully dependent on the vinedresser doing his job most effective. The ultimate production of this plant is fully dependent on the vine remaining healthy and being the source for the branches and production of the plant.

If the vinedresser were not available, then the plant would suffer tremendously. If the vine were not available, then the plant's production and fruit would die off. Both the vinedresser and vine are critical if the plant is to grow or produce anything.

The vinedresser is God the Father. The vine is Jesus Christ. And, together these two ensure that the Holy Spirit (the sap in the vine) works through the plant to produce great fruit.

As a born-again child of God, we have the vinedresser, the vine and the sap in the plant working for us, with us and in us. God has provided no less than the entire Trinity to work with and through each believer.

Has it ever occurred to you that when you pray, work, sing, serve, worship, give, fellowship and help, the entire Trinity is at work on your behalf?! Yes…that's right, the vine, the vinedresser and the sap working through the tree. They are all working for you!

FINAL THOUGHT: Read through John 15:1-8 several times. Consider jotting down ways in which the vine, the vinedresser and the sap of the vine are working on your behalf.

DAY 2: Removing that Branch
John 15:2
"Every branch in me that does not bear fruit he takes away, and every branch that does bear fruit he prunes, that it may bear more fruit."

Jesus spoke in agricultural terms. The people of that era would have understood these terms intimately. The people of Jesus' time would understand the agricultural terminology in the same way that current populations would appreciate words like gigabytes, Instagram, Snapchat and Facebook.

Jesus used an image of a conscientious farmer and what he would do to see his crop produce effectively. A farmer must eliminate that which pulls his plants down and expends their energy without product. An effective farmer would pull away the limbs that appear to be part of the plant, but are actually non-functioning, life draining appendages. These ineffective limbs and branches, once removed, allow more of the plant's life-giving nutrients to be channeled to the limbs which are producing effectively.

In spring semester my senior year, I had only one required class left to fulfill graduation expectations. That one class was senior literature. And yet, it was necessary that I fill my schedule to cover six periods. I was forced to fill my day with ceramics, PE, early release and foods (you got it…a class where we cooked everday!). One other class I took was horticulture. We studied plants. And, we were tasked with growing a plant throughout the semester.

My plant of choice was what is known as an "Inchplant" or "Wandering Jew." This plant has a solid central vine with strands that grow off of it and can be several feet in length. The Wandering Jew is a plant that is tough and hard to kill. To get the plant to grow effectively I watered it regularly and gave it plant food. One other part of tending to the plant was snipping pieces off that were simply sucking nutrients but not growing effectively.

My horticulture teacher explained to me that, if I would remove the pieces on the plant that were attached – but not functional – that the plant would ultimately flourish. By the end of the semester, my plant had almost outgrown its pot when I took it home.

So goes the life of a successful farmer. So goes the work of our great God. His love extends to such a degree that He will even make the tough decisions to remove that which will harm our growth. God's love extends to such a degree that, not only will he remove that which harms our personal growth (sometimes the removal is tough for us and for God) but also that which harms our church's growth. When God removes that which hinders growth, it opens up all the other avenues for the Holy Spirit to work even more powerfully. The removal of the dead pieces might seem difficult to you, but know that God does this out of a deep love for you.

FINAL THOUGHT: Think of things in your past that God removed, and it was painful for you and yet ultimately beneficial. Spend time praising God for His great love for you in that He loves you enough to make the tough calls!

DAY 3: STAY CONNECTED!
John 15:3-4
"Already you are clean because of the word that I have spoken to you. Abide in me, and I in you. As the branch cannot bear fruit by itself, unless it abides in the vine, neither can you, unless you abide in me."

Jesus gave a visual illustration of the way the Holy Spirit works through believers by explaining the way the vine sends nutrients through a branch. The branch has nutrients flow through it from the vine, and the vine sends the nutrients through the branch. As the vine sends the nutrients and power through the branch, then fruit is an outflow of the branch itself.

The critical piece of the branch is not to try to get nutrients. The critical piece of the branch is not to try to produce the nutrients. The critical piece of the branch is not to try to convince the vine to send nutrients.

There is only one primary goal of the branch. That is to stay connected to and remain in the vine. If the branch will do this one simple act – remain, stay connected, continue in – the vine, the vine will happily send the nutrition and power through the branch. As the vine sends this beautiful, wonderful, nutritious and vibrant sap, fruit will be an outflow of the branch. The branch is simply "remaining" in the trunk (vine).

One of my favorite tools in my set is my DeWalt 20-volt cordless drill. I can tighten and loosen screws, bolts and other fasteners much quicker than with a traditional screwdriver or wrench.

For that cordless drill, I have 30-40 different types of power tips for flathead screws, Philips head screws, bolts, Allen screws and many more. And though these tips are the pieces that actually turn the screws, they are not what makes the work happen. The motor in the drill produces the power that turns the head that makes the power tips tighten and loosen screws. The drill produces the power, and those metal tips need only to stay locked into the drill.

If you are God's child, you do not actually produce the power to live a victorious life, serve victoriously or worship victoriously. If you are God's Child, it is God and His power who actually do that work. Much like the power tips on the drill, your job is to stay and remain connected so that the true source can work through you.

If you are victorious as a believer, it will be because you have remained and continued in the Vine – Jesus Christ. If you experience a victorious Christian life, it will be because you have remained connected to the Vine which has lived through you by the Holy Spirit. The Holy Spirit is God working through you to produce the outward life of Jesus Christ. STAY CONNECTED! THAT IS ALL!

FINAL THOUGHT: Spend some time thinking through and prayerfully considering whether you have, moment by moment, learned to abide in Christ. As you learn this, the Holy Spirit will work His supernatural power through you.

DAY 4: APART FROM ME…
John 15:5
"I am the vine; you are the branches. Whoever abides in me and I in him, he it is that bears much fruit, for apart from me you can do nothing."

Jesus was fully aware that breaking a branch off of the main vine (or trunk) would essentially render the branch useless. As he (and his audience) walked mentally through a vineyard, they could see branch after branch that no longer were connected to the main vine. These branches were dried up and dead, though, on the outside, these disconnected branches may have appeared adequate – or even effective. Disconnected from the vine rendered the branches useless.

The reality that Jesus knew, and that the people around him in an agrarian society knew, was that branches separate from the main vine simply could do nothing. They could not produce. They could not grow. They could not flourish. The branches disconnected from the vine could not even keep themselves alive. There was nothing quite so dependent on everything as was a branch to the vine.

AND SO GOD'S PEOPLE. We are completely dependent on our source – Jesus Christ – for life, power, ministry, worship, spiritual production, spiritual growth or effective living.

"…apart from me you can do nothing."

A friend of mine and his family took their fifth wheel camper to the mountains to camp and enjoy nature one weekend. They found a campground with electrical hookups and stopped there. My friend is one of the more intelligent people I know, and he is a highly qualified engineer. There are few things related to mechanics, electronics or technology that he cannot repair or build.

He and his family got set up in their luxury fifth wheel camper and began to enjoy the lake, the surrounding mountains and the woods. They started a fire, fished in the lake and had a great time, until he realized that his luxurious fifth wheel had lost power.

With all of his expertise, my friend went to work. He pulled out a portable diagnostic kit he had brought with his tools and tested outlets and compressors. He crawled into the breaker area and tested each individual section. He flipped switches and performed every test he knew to perform. He could not fix the problem and he was at his wits end. He put his diagnostic equipment up in the truck, walked around the camper and realized that it had simply been unplugged from the campground outlet.

That's right. He had spent almost two hours trying to fix something that was simply disconnected. His wife really enjoyed telling that story.

No matter the complexity of your spiritual resources or your abilities, you will accomplish nothing for eternity or spiritual victory when disconnected from the Vine.

FINAL THOUGHT: Do you seek, moment by moment, to walk, talk, pray, study and learn as an outward manifestation of Jesus Christ? Only He, through His Holy Spirit in you, will ever accomplish anything real or eternal.

DAY 5: Who Gets the Glory?
John 15:8
"By this my Father is glorified, that you bear much fruit and so prove to be my disciples."

Bearing fruit in a vineyard brings attention to the farmer who tends and keeps his crop. The success of a vineyard does not bring attention to the leaves, the branches, the sap, the ground around it or the bugs on the plants. The success of a vineyard brings attention to the one who owns the vines.

Jesus, making spiritual application from an agricultural image, points out that His Father (i.e. the Vinedresser) is ultimately glorified when much fruit is produced. My calling as a believer is to stay connected and remain in the Vine. Through me, my Savior Jesus Christ will produce great fruit by the outworking of His Holy Spirit. As the Holy Spirit works through me and produces much fruit, it is the Vinedresser who receives the attention.

The spiritual fruit produced in my life is not for the attention of the "branch" but of the Vinedresser. If you attempt to produce "spiritual fruit" in such a way that you gain the attention of people, it is wax fruit. Activity that looks spiritual, but brings attention to the "branch," is false and without any real benefit. The true fruit brings attention and glory to the Vinedresser, Almighty God.

In the early 2000s Emily Thompson traveled to New York City with her Masters degree in art. Her focus had been sculpture. She began as an assistant to a sculptor in his studio.

Along the way, some family members asked her about doing flowers for a wedding. That job led into several more, which, in turn, led into a full-blown career and focus on floral art.

Now, Emily Thompson is a world-renowned florist with clients such as Google, Architectural Digest, MAC Cosmetics and the White House. Each of Thompson's floral displays is unique, magnificent and bringing greater attention to her. She is the florist (the vinedresser if you will), and it is to her that the attention for these remarkable floral designs goes.

That makes sense. Thompson does the work and Thompson gets the glory for her work.

In Christ, God indwells each believer with His Holy Spirit. As the Holy Spirit works through each believer, the Christian's only job is to stay vitally connected. The work of the Holy Spirit through each believer will produce spiritual fruit that will ultimately bring attention and glory to the one whose work is on display – Jesus the Savior and our Father in heaven. May we bear much fruit that our God may be most glorified!

FINAL THOUGHT: List out some things in your life that you know God has done. Now, spend time in praise and adoration to Him for His work through you.

The Perfect Counselor Study Guide: Week 5

1. In your own words, re-write John 15:1.

2. What is the process Jesus is describing in John 15:2?

3. How could John 15:2 relate to what John writes in 1John 2:19?

4. What kind of fruit is John discussing? Take a look at these passages to see various kinds of spiritual fruit. The Bible seems to exhibit spiritual fruit amongst believers that is sometimes action/activities, and sometimes the fruit is more about attitude. About by each passage write whether you think this spiritual fruit described is action fruit or attitude fruit.

   a. Acts 2:38-41
   b. Acts 4:32
   c. Acts 9:31
   d. Romans 1:8
   e. Romans 1:11-12
   f. Galatians 5:22-23

5. According to John 15:3 Jesus described the disciples as having already been made clean by "the word that I have spoken to you." With that statement, what was Jesus saying about the spiritual position of His closest disciples?

6. From Jesus' statements in John 15:3-4, we see his reference to "the branch" (each Christian) and the vine (Jesus). What is the primary job of the branch in this relationship?

7. According to the first phrase in John 15:8, as believers bear spiritual fruit (both attitude and action), what does this outflow do relative to God?

8. The fruit production discussed John 15:8, not only glorifies God but proves what to the world?

9. Jesus explains in John 15:8 that producing spiritual fruit, not only glorifies God but also proves the discipleship of His people to the world. How does this idea of glorifying God and demonstrating discipleship relate to Matthew 22:37-39?

THE PERFECT COUNSELOR DEVOTIONS: WEEK 6
Alone with God

DAY 1: It's His Fruit

Galatians 5:22-23

"But the fruit of the Spirit is love, joy, peace, patience, kindness, goodness, faithfulness, gentleness, self-control; against such things there is no law."

The Apostle Paul, in an effort to explain what it looks like when a born-again believer lives in the power of the Holy Spirit, uses an agricultural image – a little like Jesus did. His image is of a fruit orchard and the trees that produce that fruit. Paul's description was of the outgrowth of a fruit tree.

Once the nutrients of a tree are sucked up from the roots and through the vine, they are dispersed out through the branches. The nutrients work out through the branches and produce fruit. The fruit is the work of the farmer and vine working together.

The fruit is essentially a by-product of an effectively working tree. If there is no fruit, then the tree vine and roots were not working together well. If there is no fruit, then it is not the fruit's fault, for the fruit is a by-product of the effective inward working of the tree. The fruit of the tree is not the main working of the tree, but it is the proof that the main part of the tree is working well.

Years ago, when my family lived in a church-owned home, we were told that there was a persimmon tree that had been planted in the backyard years earlier by a former pastor. I looked and looked for a persimmon tree but could not find one.

I was no horticultural expert (and still am not), but I knew what a persimmon looked like. It was the time of the season for the persimmons to produce, so I felt that I could easily pick out the tree that way. I looked for a tree that had persimmons on it, but none were to be found.

Finally, I asked one of our ladies in the church where the persimmon tree would be. The house was next door to the church, so she walked across the parking lot with me and showed me the tree. I chuckled out loud because it was a small, shriveled-up tree with one, small, dried-up persimmon hanging on it. And, as she and I quickly learned, that persimmon tree was eventually dead. The problem was not with the fruit, but the problem was with the inner workings of that plant.

Every single Christian has been placed in the Holy Spirit, and the Holy Spirit has been placed in him. The Holy Spirit is the power of Jesus, and if He is living through us, He will produce His fruit. If spiritual fruit is not evident in the life of the believer, then the problem is not with the outward fruit (attitudes and behaviors) but with the working of the Spirit inwardly. IF YOU ARE WALKING IN THE POWER OF THE HOLY SPIRIT, HE WILL PRODUCE HIS FRUIT THROUGH YOUR LIFE! I GUARANTEE IT!

FINAL THOUGHT: Practice the presence of God moment by moment today, asking God to – by faith – to fill and lead you by His Holy Spirit. Moment by moment is how spiritual fruit is produced.

DAY 2: My Display
Galatians 5:22-23
"But the fruit of the Spirit is love, joy, peace, patience, kindness, goodness, faithfulness, gentleness, self-control; against such things there is no law."

As Paul used the image of the fruit tree, he understood in explaining it that the fruit of the tree was an outgrowth from the inner workings of that tree. He also understood that fruit produced by a tree would be easily identifiable. The fruit produced by the Holy Spirit through the life of a Christian is obvious. It is "love, joy, peace, patience, kindness, goodness, faithfulness, gentleness, self-control..." This fruit will be clear from the believer and to the outside world

Apple trees are clearly identifiable. Orange trees are clearly identifiable. Pear trees are clearly identifiable. The same can be said for most all fruit trees. It is clear, based on the fruit they have hanging, what type of tree one is seeing. External fruit will expose the type of tree that it is.

Suppose I wanted an apple tree, but all I had was a pear tree? If I picked all of the pears off of the pear tree, and then proceeded to fasten apples to the ends of the branches, would that then make that tree an apple tree? Of course not. A tree will produce the fruit that is consistent with its inner workings.

Suppose I wanted an orange tree, but all I had was an apple tree? Would removing the oranges and hanging apples on that tree make it an orange tree? Of course not. That orange tree, consistent with its inner workings, would produce oranges.

The fruit that is expressed outwardly in the lives of believers will be consistent with the inner workings happening in that person. If the Holy Spirit is at work through me, His fruit will be produced. If the flesh is at work in me, the works of the flesh will be produced. Ultimately, a Christian can say a lot about what is at work in them, but the external fruit will display what is really working on the inside.

If the fruit of your life is displaying impatience, then what is working inside is not the Holy Spirit.

If the fruit of your life is displaying anger, bitterness and unforgiveness, then what is working on the inside is not the Holy Spirit.

If the fruit of your life is displaying anxiety (no peace), dissatisfaction and pessimism (no joy), conflict (no gentleness) and self-indulgence (no self-control), then I can be certain that the Holy Spirit is not the one working on the inside of you.

The fruit of your life will make it quite clear to anyone watching who and what are working inside of you.

FINAL THOUGHT: If you find that the fruit of the Spirit is not what seems to be expressed outwardly, then the key is not to run around trying to produce it but to be more intimately involved with the One who does produce it. Your intimacy and love relationship with Jesus Christ will make all the difference in walking in the Spirit. Walking in the power of the Holy Spirit will ultimately determine the fruit production of your life.

DAY 3: CRUCIFIED!

Galatians 5:24

"And those who belong to Christ Jesus have crucified the flesh with its passions and desires."

As the Apostle Paul has used the agricultural image of the fruit trees, he now moves into more of a spiritual application. The fruit tree idea transitions into personal, spiritual action.

Not only does Paul move from illustration to application, but he moves from one tree to another. From fruit tree to the cross. From display of the Spirit's outward work to an explanation of how He accomplishes the hard work – the cross.

And, even as the people of that day would understand agriculture, they would also understand crucifixion. Crucifixion was a symbol of death. The cross was a symbol of execution. The Roman Empire had perfected the art of horrid executions. When the cross was involved in a situation, death was always involved. When the cross was applied in a criminal's life, everyone in its path would end up dead.

In Galatians 5:24 it is the born-again child of God who is the subject of the statement, but the flesh is the object of the verb "crucified." The flesh, Paul declares, was crucified – past tense. At the moment of conversion, each believer experienced a death and a resurrection. The lost person is controlled by a sin nature that prevents him or her from following God, but at conversion, Christ's work on the cross is applied, and the "old man" is put to death. In a sense, that old sin nature is "crucified" with Christ on the cross (when Christ was crucified, it was done for everyone who would ever believe).

Now, as the born-again believer walks through life, he or she walks by faith in the knowledge that the power of the old nature is dead. That said, each believe still fights against the old tendencies. Those old tendencies (or how we cope with life apart from the power of the Holy Spirit) are "the flesh." And though that flesh has been "crucified," (put to death) it sometimes still causes the believer to gravitate toward it.

When the believer acknowledges the flesh as "crucified," and walks by faith in that knowledge, he or she is in the place for the Holy Spirit (the living Christ) to walk through him. As a believer walks in the power of the Holy Spirit, then she is walking by the living power of Jesus Christ through her life. It is as if these bodies are simply a costume in need of animating, and when we walk crucified to the flesh, the Holy Spirit makes them alive by His power. When this happens (crucifying the flesh and being alive in the Holy Spirit), then the Holy Spirit produces the life of Christ in these mortal bodies — and He produces the spiritual fruit.

So what about you? Will you keep trying to manufacture the fruit of your efforts or learn to allow the Holy Spirit to live through you...as one whose flesh has been put to death?

FINAL THOUGHT: A person simply cannot manufacture and produce that which only Jesus can make. A person simply cannot produce what only the Holy Spirit can. And yet, when the Holy Spirit is living His life through us, He will produce things we could never have imagined possible.

DAY 4: An Explosion and A Slow Burn
Galatians 5:25
"If we live by the Spirit, let us also keep in step with the Spirit."

As Paul continued his conversation challenging the Galatians to walk in the same grace in which they had been converted, he makes a declaration that is both a statement and a command. The introductory statement Paul makes "If we live by the Spirit" can also be read as "since we live by the Spirit" (NIV).

Paul's statement here is acknowledging the life we have as believers in the Holy Spirit of God. Romans 6:3-5 explains that Christ's death was accomplished that we might also put to death our old sin nature. Not only that, but in the same way we were united in His death, we are also united in His life. It is the Holy Spirit in each believer that gives us that life in us.

At the moment of conversion, every Christian is united in His death (forgiveness of sin) and His life (baptized in the Holy Spirit). This same Holy Spirit who gives us new life at conversion also provides us the daily capability to live and walk out this life.

The same explosive life of Jesus in which we were baptized at conversion is the same sustaining power that lives through us moment by moment to love our spouse.

The same sudden burst of life-giving energy that the Holy Spirit provided at conversion is the same source of energy that gently flows through us to raise our children.

The same Holy Spirit who invades us at conversion is also steadily trickling through us each day to love one another.

The same Holy Spirit who overtakes us at our justification is the same power to gradually, steadily and incrementally change us in sanctification.

The Holy Spirit immersed you at conversion, and He continues to work through you daily to glorify God at work, worship God with your daily activities, serve God in your local church, witness to God in your community and systematically point people to God with the fruit of the Spirit.

It was the Holy Spirit who enveloped you at your conversion. He is the same one making it possible now to live out Christ day by day.

The Holy Spirit was a mighty explosion at conversion, and He is now a slow burn in you day to day.

At conversion, the Holy Spirit was a lightning bolt who provided an enormous collision of spiritual electricity to completely and radically change your life.

Daily, the Holy Spirit is a steady flow of electricity to charge your batteries, enable your love, exercise your energy and fill you to overflowing.

Since you were born again by the sudden invasion of the Holy Spirit, you are now spiritually breathing, walking and having your heart pumped by His flow.

FINAL THOUGHT: Take on the challenge to memorize Galatians 5:16 and Galatians 5:25.

DAY 5: Try Not to Think About Pink Elephants!
Galatians 5:26
"Let us not become conceited, provoking one another, envying one another."

At first glance, given the subject of verses 22-25, it would appear that the Apostle Paul has gone off topic in verse 26. While discussing the imagery of fruit and transitioning to the idea of crucifixion in a way that ties the two seamlessly together, he suddenly issues a startling proclamation: Let us not become conceited, provoking one another, envying one another.

And yet, what seems to be a sudden lurch into the ditch makes complete sense in the context. In verses 22-23, all of the spiritual fruits described are character traits of those whose lives are completely unfocused on self. All nine elements of spiritual fruit emanate from a place of selfless expressions of Jesus. In verse 24, once again, Paul is speaking to the Galatians and describing a selfless life whereby personal flesh patterns, personal passions and personal desires are crucified – put to death. This is another declaration of war on selfishness.

Finally, verse 25 is the culmination of verses 22-24, in that selflessly living out the life of Jesus and the Holy Spirit will take place as we live by His power. It is the moment by moment death-to-self, and yielded heart to Jesus that allows the Holy Spirit to live through us and reproduce the life of Jesus in us.

It is no wonder then that, after having spent so much time explaining the look of a selfless life, Paul confronts selfish behavior that must have been rearing its ugly head in the church. The opposite of selfless is selfish. The counterpunch to death-to-self and alive to Jesus if full-of-self and tone deaf to the Spirit of Jesus.

So then the question: How does one avoid the selfishness proclaimed in 5:26? He does it by fulfilling the calling of 22-25 (actually 5:16-25). Living a life that avoids selfish behavior and exudes the Spirit of Jesus is accomplished, not by thinking a lot about the selfish behavior, but by putting most stock and thought in yielding to Jesus.

If I tell you: Do not think about pink elephants!

Most likely you just thought about pink elephants. The best way to avoid thinking of those pink elephants, is not to fill your mind with the avoidance of pink elephants. The best way to avoid thinking of those pink pachyderms is to fill your mind with something completely different. When I fill my mind with something else, then I need not worry about it being filled with the thing I am to avoid.

And so my life. If I do not want to see my life filled with selfish behavior, then I allow my life to be filled with that which is selfless. If I do not want my life filled with negative, self-centered, flesh-patterned attitudes and behaviors, then my best bet is to fill it up with the power and presence of the Holy Spirit – the life of Jesus. The more I am emptied of self and filled with the Holy Spirit (which, unlike spiritual baptism, is a daily activity), the less room I leave for selfish behavior, or being full of self.

FINAL THOUGHT: Consider starting each day, even before leaving bed, with this brief prayer: Lord, fill me with your Spirit today and produce the life of Jesus through me. Then, by faith and moment by moment, start into your day with the knowledge that God is faithful to do that.

The Perfect Counselor Study Guide: Week 6

. Take a moment and, without looking it up, think about what a working definition of "fruit" is. At this point, do not think in terms of spiritual fruit, but just fruit in general. Write that definition down.

. In Galatians 5:22-23 we see nine aspects of fruit exhibited from those who are controlled by the Holy Spirit. Below, out beside each fruit, write another word for it.

  a. Love
  b. Joy
  c. Peace
  d. Patience
  e. Kindness
  f. Goodness
  g. Faithfulness
  h. Gentleness
  i. Self-control

. What final comment does Paul make regarding the fruit of the Spirit?

. Read through Galatians 5:24. What part does the flesh have in this production of spiritual fruit?

. Consider Matthew 10:38, Matthew 16:24 and Luke 9:23. In what way do these verses relate to the declaration in Galatians 5:24.

. Continuing on to Galatians 5:25, Paul speaks of the condition of a believer being enabled to "live by the Spirit." In this verse, "If" can also easily be translated "Since". Write the verse out using "Since" instead of "If".

7. Since a Christian is made alive (or, lives) by the Spirit, Paul declares that the normal behavior is then that we would do what?

8. Consider these additional ideas of the Bible's call to Christians in terms of ongoing spiritual life. For each verse, in a sentence or two, describe what it is calling Christians to do.

a. Romans 13:14
b. Ephesians 5:18
c. Colossians 2:6
d. Colossians 2:12

I have written all about it, but every time I get there it seems like God just kind of washes over me again with: Are you doing this, John? Are you living by the Spirit? Are you bearing the fruit of the Spirit? Are you keeping in step with the Spirit? And I have to just pause and say, "Oh, God, I can do so much better. I want so much to enjoy fellowship with you in the leading of the Spirit."

> – John Piper,
> Desiring God
> Ministries

DAY 1: Gold Plated…or Just Gold?

1Corinthians 12:1-3

"Now concerning spiritual gifts, brothers, I do not want you to be uninformed. You know that when you were pagans you were led astray to mute idols; however you were led.   Therefore, I want you to understand that no one speaking in the Spirit of God ever says 'Jesus is accursed!' and no one can say 'Jesus is Lord' except in the Holy Spirit."

As the Apostle Paul explains to the Corinthians how the Holy Spirit and His giftings to believers work, he reminds them of their worship prior to salvation. Their worship of false idols was what drove them and their lives. In the same way, they have given themselves over completely to Christ.

And, in fact, Paul explains that the Holy Spirit in them is the only one who can truly enable believers to declare honestly that Jesus is Lord. The word "Lord" means master, ruler, king and authority. If a person has yielded his or her life to Jesus as complete Lord, then the omnipotent Father has placed in them His Holy Spirit. It is the Holy Spirit in a believer that allows that believer to honestly say Jesus is his Master. And, conversely, if the Holy Spirit is not in a person, then Jesus cannot be his Lord – and thus, he cannot call him Lord.

Once, in Oahu, Hawaii, the news reported that a group was presenting itself as stranded, hard luck tourists and selling jewelry that looked like real gold but was fake. According to the news report, this European Gypsy caravan was telling people that they had been stranded on the island, needed to get home and would sell their valuable gold jewelry – worth thousands of dollars – for merely hundreds.

The gullible people who purchased the jewelry got it home and discovered that it was not really gold. It only looked like gold on the outside, but the inside was other types of fake metal.

No matter how much someone claims jewelry to be real gold, if the inside of that jewelry does not contain gold, then it is fake. What is on the inside of that jewelry will ultimately determine whether it is what the seller says it is.

When a person claims that Jesus is his or her Lord, it can only be true if the Holy Spirit of God is on the inside of him at work. At the point of a person's conversion, God forgives him or her, declares him righteous and prepares a place in heaven. In addition, the new believer is baptized into the Holy Spirit of God. He is placed in them and they in Him. In this way, only a person with the Holy Spirit in them can say Jesus is Lord, and only a person truly saying Jesus is Lord has the Holy Spirit inside of them.

Take heart child of God! If you are truly born again, the one you call Lord is living inside of you through His Holy Spirit.

FINAL THOUGHT: Think back to a time when you were truly born again. That was the point where the Holy Spirit of God was placed in you. And, if Jesus is not truly Lord of your life, then the Holy Spirit does not truly live in you.

DAY 2: THE PAST!

1Corinthians 12:1-3

'Now concerning spiritual gifts, brothers, I do not want you to be uninformed. You know that when you were pagans you were led astray to mute idols; however you were led. Therefore, I want you to understand that no one speaking in the Spirit of God ever says, 'Jesus is accursed!' and no one can say 'Jesus is Lord' except in the Holy Spirit."

The Apostle Paul brings up the Corinthian's past. He references the leadership of their lives, and it was idolatry. These Corinthians had been followers and worshippers of idols.

Why would Paul take them back to the dark days of worshiping false gods? Why would Paul make them think back to those days without hope, without Christ and without a true Savior – only false idols?

One might ask Paul, "Is there ever a good time to cause God's children to think back to the aimless, lost days prior to their salvation?" And, obviously, the answer from Paul would be yes. The evidence of his words in this passage displays Paul's willingness to force the thoughts of God's children back to the days of darkness and idolatry.

Yet, are God's children not to move on from the past? "All things made new." and all of that...right? And still we are held with the idea that the Apostle Paul, right in the middle of his letter that is God-breathed Scripture, compels the Corinthians to think of their past. Must have been a very good reason!

Paul is not urging the Corinthians to dwell on the past, but to contrast their unregenerate past with their sanctified present. Leveraging the past to celebrate and grow in the present is a completely valid step for any believer.

Dwelling on my past in a way that fills me with guilt and regret? A bad idea!

Dwelling on my past to remember the bad things I did as if they were still statements of condemnation against me now? TERRIBLE IDEA!

Thinking temporarily about how my dark past contrasts with my hope-filled present and hopeful future? GREAT IDEA!

Some might say that it is difficult to fully appreciate your present salvation without being reminded of just how hopeless you were prior to conversion. Your present looks better and better when you grasp the horror, hopelessness and despair of your past.

In my possession, I have a cassette tape (yes…a cassette tape..) of the first sermon I ever preached in August of 1989. Several years ago I had it converted to a CD format, so I could listen to it periodically. I am the only one who has ever listened to the recording. It is a poor sermon. It is 16 minutes long. It takes the passage out of context. The application is poorly stated. In that first sermon, I used one story as an illustration, and I really did not tell it that well.

Nevertheless, periodically, I pull out that first sermon and listen. I listen for no other reason than to thank God that He has helped me make progress. I still am learning how to preach, but thank God I am not where I began! Do not ever stay stuck in your past, but glance at your past that you might never forget how far God has brought you today!

FINAL THOUGHT: Make a list of some areas where God has changed you since before you were saved. Take some time to praise Him for what He has done!

DAY 3: Dem Bones!
1Corinthians 12:4-6
"Now there are varieties of gifts, but the same Spirit; and there are varieties of service, but the same Lord; and there are varieties of activities, but it is the same God who empowers them all in everyone.

Even as the Apostle Paul, in verses 1-3, described the Lordship the Holy Spirit establishes in every believer, in verses 4-6 he goes on to explain the oneship. As each believer is baptized into the Holy Spirit at conversion (Acts 1:5; 1Corinthians 12:13), this common immersion makes us one who are many.

Paul begins to describe the way in which God's people are varied but one. He asserts the idea that, though we are all one in the Holy Spirit, we also are gifted and enabled by that same Holy Spirit in a variety of ways.

Part of the great beauty of the church is that what makes us different as we enter the church is inferior to what makes us one. And yet, without our differences, we could not really be unified. A group of people who are together and all the same is a display of uniformity, but not unity. A group of unique people of different races, ethnicities, skills, personalities and abilities who are made one by the Holy Spirit is a display of unity.

Paul describes this unity by using gifts, service and activities in their plural forms. He also uses Spirit, Lord and God in singular forms. The plural elements are the uniqueness of each believer, and the singular elements are the unity of those same varies members. These varied elements and expressions of each believer make them unique but contribute to the one, unified mosaic that is the church.

Child of God, you are made one in the church – not in spite of your uniqueness – but because of your uniqueness. Child of God celebrate your diversity that God has crafted and participate in the unity that Christ has won at the cross. The Holy Spirit comes into your life at conversion to make you part of a varied and beautiful puzzle that is the local church. Each unique piece is put in place, and it creates one picturesque scene. Each piece placed in the body is distinctive, diverse and extraordinary. All these exceptional pieces are placed together in the Holy Spirit to make an irreplaceable whole in the church.

At birth, the human body has 270 individual bones, which become 206 at adulthood, because of bones fusing together (www.sciencing.com, October 29, 2018). Each of these bones is unique and has distinctive purposes. Bringing these bones together, with central nervous and cardiovascular systems, makes them unified and work together. They remain distinct ("Toe bone connected to the foot bone Foot bone connected to the heel bone, Heel bone connected to the ankle bone…") but unified in a common purpose.

And so the local church of Jesus Christ. All the varied types of people come together and are made family and unified by the Holy Spirit in us. Celebrate your diversity, but at the same time, celebrate your unity in the church. The Holy Spirit has made it that way.

FINAL THOUGHT: Meditate for a few minutes on the diverse gifts you bring to the church. Meditate also on how your diverse gifts are being used in the church to fulfill the common purpose.

DAY 4: Gifts, Services and Activities
1Corinthians 12:4-6
'Now there are varieties of gifts, but the same Spirit; and there are varieties of service, but the same Lord; and there are varieties of activities, but it is the same God who empowers them all in everyone."

Gifts   (noun)

- a thing given willingly to someone without payment; a present.
- something voluntarily transferred by one person to another without compensation

(verb)

- to endow with some power, quality, or attribute

Service (noun)

- the occupation or function of serving
- contribution to the welfare of others

Activities

- a pursuit in which a person is active
- a process (such as digestion) that an organism carries on or participates in by virtue of being alive

Paul mentions three specific elements God adds to the life of each born again believer the moment he or she is converted. While each of these elements is a different category, each accomplishes the work of glorifying Christ and edifying the church.

Gifts are bestowed on every believer by a benevolent, gracious, merciful God. And while these gifts were paid for by the body and blood of our precious Savior Jesus, Christians owe nothing for them. They are gifts to enable us to fulfill the purpose of glorifying God and edifying man.

Services are granted to every believer that we might have something to give back. These services are not given by believers to repay God, but they are given out by believers that we might emulate the attitude and behavior of Christ. Once a believer gives his or her life away to Christ, he receives much more back to give away to others with no expectation of anything in return.

Activities are everyday life experiences that are common to each believer. These are not extraordinary actions, but mundane activities. These activities, at the point of conversion, become opportunities for eternal impact by the believer rather than simply boring behaviors. In other words, at my conversion my average daily activities up to that point were transformed by Christ to eternity impacting routines.

Look up child of God! God has given you gifts to glorify Him, services to pour into others and mundane behaviors that help turn to the lost to Him! FINAL THOUGHT: Think back on yesterday. As much as you are able, write down an hour by hour list of your schedule from then. Now, spend time praising God for how he may have used it for His glory.

DAY 5: You Are an "Each."
1Corinthians 12:7
"To each is given the manifestation of the Spirit for the common good."

Each who? Each what? Paul here is speaking of each member of the Body of Christ. He is speaking, not of only the "special Christians" or the Super Saints, but also of every single believer who has lived, is living and will live in the future.

You are a child of God? You are not exempt from this "each."

You are an anonymous follower of Christ? You are included in this "each."

You are an introverted church member? You are included in this "each."

You are a believer who slips in late to worship, sits in the back row (or balcony) and are terrified of the "fellowship" time in the middle of the service? You are included in this "each."

Not only is every believer included in this each, every single believer also has a personal stake in the common good. The common good is the overall health and success of the local church. Ladies and gentlemen, if you are born again, you are part of that success…no matter how insignificant…or significant…you think you might be.

There is a story of a lady who had been active in her local church in many areas as she served the Lord. She did many things well but played the piano especially well. One day she became confined to her house because of a serious illness. She knew that, though she could not do much, she could still play.

She posted an ad on social media and in the local newspaper that read: Will play special requests for Christian praise music and worship songs. Call the number listed below."

She posted the ads and waited. Within a couple of days, she was receiving phones calls throughout the day to play songs of worship and faith.

That lady was surely one of the "each."

If you are truly a child of God through Jesus Christ, He has manifested Himself in your life in a way that will allow you to do ministry that contributes to the "common good." You are not small enough, short enough, unknown enough, untalented enough, unable enough, or just plain unremarkable enough to be exempted from the "each."

You must embrace the fact that, as a born-again child of God, you have been given a manifestation of Jesus Christ that He wants you to use. In fact, the future success and progress of the church is related to how "each's" like you utilize the manifestations God has given you to contribute.

Do not ever, for one second, think that you are without a manifestation of Christ to contribute to the success of the church – unless, of course, you are completely without Christ and have never truly been converted. And...well...that is another discussion entirely. But, if you are a child of God, then you are an "each." Discover the "each" that you are and serve the Lord!

FINAL THOUGHT: Look up, child of God! Christ wants to use you. Prayerfully consider this: Lord, how am I currently being used to advance the ministry and mission of the church where I am involved?

The Perfect Counselor Study Guide: Week 7

1. Read through 1Corinthians 1:4-9. What does the Apostle Paul seem to be saying about the gifts that the Corinthian Christians possess?

2. The Apostle Paul begins to address spiritual gifts in 1Corinthians 12.

    a. These spiritual gifts are enablements the Holy Spirit gives to born-again believers to glorify Christ and edify the church. These are the spiritual gifts or the gifts OF THE SPIRIT. In other words, these gifts are actually possessed by the Holy Spirit. What is the significance of Paul stating that, while these gifts are given to us, they are gifts possessed by the Holy Spirit?

    b. As Paul speaks in 1Corinthians 12:1, what is his first concern about the Corinthians and their gifts?

3. As Paul lays out his instruction to the Corinthian Church in 1Corinthians 12:2, he first reminds them of where they once were. What specific element of their past lives does he mention?

4. While every Christian needs to understand that living in our past is not healthy for spiritual growth, below, share at least two reasons our past can be helpful in growing spiritually in the present:

5. In 1Corinthians 12:3, Paul points out what it looks like when a person is empowered and led by the Holy Spirit. Below, give 2-3 statements on what it looks like in a believer's life when we honestly say, "Jesus is Lord."

6. As Paul describes spiritual gifts in 1Corinthians 12:4-6, there are three varieties. List those three below, and in your own words, describe

---

what you think each means (Hint – Use a Bible app to compare the wording of these three "varieties" with differing translations).

7. In addition to the three varieties mentioned in 1Corinthians 12:4-6, what are the three elements that make them the same? Also, what is significant about these three statements of unity? (Hint: See Matthew 28:19)

8. Ultimately, according to Paul's instruction in 1Corinthians 12:7, what is the "end game" for utilizing these spiritual gifts?

THE PERFECT COUNSELOR DEVOTIONS: WEEK 8
Alone with God

DAY 1: Which Part?

1Corinthians 12:8-10

"For to one is given through the Spirit the utterance of wisdom, and to another the utterance of knowledge according to the same Spirit, to another faith by the same Spirit, to another gifts of healing by the one Spirit, to another the working of miracles, to another prophecy, to another the ability to distinguish between spirits, to another various kinds of tongues, to another the interpretation of tongues."

Utterance of wisdom:	A ministry to uphold deep biblical wisdom for the local church.
Utterance of knowledge:	A ministry to uphold true biblical study for the local church.
Faith:	A ministry to uphold supernatural steps for the local church.
Gifts of healing:	A ministry to verify the Gospel in pioneer territories of the local church.
Working of miracles:	A ministry to verify the Gospel in pioneer areas of the local church.
Prophecy:	A ministry to clearly proclaim truth in the local church.
Distinguish spirits:	A ministry to protect against false prophets in the local church.
Tongues & Interpretation:	A ministry to verify and share the Gospel in foreign, pioneer fields.

A batch of spiritual gifts – and that is not all of them listed in the New Testament – that fulfills a variety of ministries, efforts and outreach ministries of the local church. Every single gift has its place, and every single Christian is enabled with one of these in this list below or others like pastors, evangelists, teachers, gifts of administration, gifts of service, gifts of mercy, gifts of leading, gifts of giving, and gifts of speaking.

Each of these gifts has its place, and each of these gifts has its place of importance and influence in the local church. A person cannot be born-again and not have one or more of these spiritual gifts (or...gifts of the Holy Spirit). Furthermore, each of these gifts is used in the life of the local church to further its mission of glorifying God, equipping and discipling the saints and reaching the lost.

In a 2015 article on the StandridgeAuto.com website, titled How Many Parts Does the Average Automobile Have?, it is stated that the average number is 30,000. The average car possesses around 30,000 parts – each part with its own design, shape, function and purpose.

And, though some of those parts out of the 30,000 are more prominent than others, each part exists to help the effectiveness and function of the automobile. Each part, if it disappears, would affect the efficiency, comfort, speed or effectiveness of the car. Not only does the car work well with the 30,000 parts, but it functions effectively because of the 30,000 parts.

In Christ, each believer is placed in the Body of Christ with a particular gift and for a particular function. Each believer is to be one of God's many parts for the church to function with efficiency and effectiveness. WHAT PART ARE YOU?

FINAL THOUGHT: Prayerfully consider how you are currently serving and being used in the local church. If you find that you are not serving in specific ways, prayerfully ask God for direction on this and seek to find a place to plug in.

DAY 2: To Another

1Corinthians 12:8-10

"For to one is given through the Spirit the utterance of wisdom, and to another the utterance of knowledge according to the same Spirit, to another faith by the same Spirit, to another gifts of healing by the one Spirit, to another the working of miracles, to another prophecy, to another the ability to distinguish between spirits, to another various kinds of tongues, to another the interpretation of tongues."

The Apostle Paul walks through the litany of spiritual gifts to explain that they are given by God through the Holy Spirit. These gifts – each of them – is given "to another."

Considering what Paul explains for each gift, he seems to emphasize that each gift is given to unique individuals – to another. Paul explains that each member of that body of Christ and that fellowship have specific spiritual gifts given them by the Holy Spirit.

The truth Paul explains in this passage is a truth that is still resonating today. Every single born-again member of the local church has been equipped with a specific enablement. Not one single person who is a true member of the local church has been placed there by God without a gifting that enables them to exalt Christ and equip people. Not one single person is more important (or less) than another. Each member is equipped that he or she might fulfill a critical function for the glorifying of God, equipping the saints and reaching the lost.

One member who withdraws from a church takes his or her enablement out of the function of the church. It is as if the member who stays away from church has sidelined the spiritual gift with which God has equipped him. Any time a born-again believer stays away from regular attendance and involvement in the local church, then he or she is shelving the gift God has placed in them.

It is like choosing to drive my brand-new car with one spark plug removed and laying on the shelf all the time.

It is like choosing to type an email to a friend, but the A and J keys are removed from the keyboard.

It is like taking the stairs in an eight-story building, but three steps are missing from each floor.

It is like owning a restaurant called Great Burgers that boasts of fresh meat delivered daily, but the hamburger meat is not available at all one day a week.

In all these instances, the functions or activities can still be accomplished, but with greatly diminished effectiveness. Each individual believer has been equipped and gifted with functions that are to contribute to the effectiveness and overall ministry of the church. When any of these has chosen to go missing, then so does the gifting that God placed in them.

Can the church still function with members who have disappeared? Of course it can (and usually does), but not without a loss in effectiveness.

If you are a born-again believer, then you are one of the "to another(s)" of which Paul speaks. You have been enabled and gifted with a specific calling, ability and function. When you take that calling, ability and function and shelve it, you have just contributed to the inefficiency of the church of Jesus Christ.

But…look up child of God! When you participate in the life of the church weekly, the gift God has given you is now part of the efficient working of the Body and Bride of Christ!

FINAL THOUGHT: Do you know where God has specifically gifted you? If not, spend some time asking God to begin showing you that. If yes, then praise Him for that gift!

DAY 3: Go Straight to the Source!
1Corinthians 12:8-10
"For to one is given through the Spirit the utterance of wisdom, and to another the utterance of knowledge according to the same Spirit, to another faith by the same Spirit, to another gifts of healing by the one Spirit, to another the working of miracles, to another prophecy, to another the ability to distinguish between spirits, to another various kinds of tongues, to another the interpretation of tongues."

The Apostle Paul is quite clear to explain to the Corinthians the source of the variety of spiritual gifts that were bestowed on them. He was clear to explain the power and energy by which their gifts were given and enabled. Paul is exhibiting the idea that the source is as important to know as the expressions of the source. The source of the workings is possibly more important than the outward workings themselves.

Whether it was utterance of wisdom, utterance of knowledge, faith, healing, working of miracles, prophecy, distinguishing between spirits, tongues, or interpretation of tongues, the source of these was identical. The source of these gifts (and many others – see Romans 12 and Ephesians 4) was the same. The power, energy and source that established and implemented these gifts was the same Holy Spirit.

The reality for the Corinthian believers was that it was more critical for them to know the source than the enablements the source provided. For, if they would be plugged in to the source (the Holy Spirit), then He would produce and empower the spiritual gifts.

Which is more critical to care for season in and season out – the tree or the fruit produced by the tree? If a farmer cares well for the trees, then those trees – the source of the fruit – will produce the fruit. Certainly, an apple farmer cares for the apples produced. Certainly, an orange farmer cares for the oranges his trees produced.   Certainly, a farmer with pear trees cares for the pears that are produced.

However, apples, oranges and pears are not fundamentally as critical as the trees that produce them. If the trees are cared for well, then the fruit that they produce will come about. If the trees are kept healthy, they will produce healthy fruit. If the trees are maintained and developed well, these trees will have fruit that grows well – whether apples, oranges or pears.

As a follower of Christ, it is certainly helpful to know the gifts that God has given each of us. However, more critical than knowing the gifts is knowing the source of those gifts well. If each believer will walk in step with, and filled by, the Holy Spirit, then He will produce supernatural work through that believer.

Romans 13:14 and Galatians 5:16 both call believers to stay empowered by and in step with the Holy Spirit. As that happens, it is the Holy Spirit who will produce the gifts and empower the spiritual gifts. You may or may not know exactly what your spiritual gifts are, but starting by walking in the filling and power of the Holy Spirit is a great place to begin.

FINAL THOUGHT: Each day, prior to leaving your bed in the morning, consider possibly praying this prayer:

"Lord, fill me with Your Holy Spirit today. Empower me, and I will walk by faith in Him."

DAY 4: The Multiple Connection
1Corinthians 12:11
"All these are the work of one and the same Spirit, and he distributes them to each one, just as he determines."

Paul continues to emphasize to the Corinthians that their spiritual gifts (of which they are so proud – 1Cor. 1:4-10) were not theirs at all. In fact, the gifts given them by the Holy Spirit of God were still possessed by that same Holy Spirit. They were referred to as "spiritual gifts" or "gifts of the Spirit." In each case, Paul's use of this term revealed the possessor of those gifts. Though Christians may be the conduits of these gifts in Corinth, the owner of them is still the Holy Spirit.

The one Holy Spirit distributed the gifts as He saw fit, and that same One supplied the power for them. The power and energy to make the gifts effective came from the One who owned them and who was the source for making them work.

Paul was explaining and displaying to each Christian who the source of our gifts is and where the power for our gifts is derived. Child of God, if you are a follower of Christ, at the moment of your conversion, you were baptized in the Holy Spirit and enabled with one or more spiritual ability to be used to help fulfill the mission of the church and glorify God.

This gift was graciously given to you by the same Holy Spirit who came to indwell you at conversion. This gift is now graciously enabled and empowered by the same Holy Spirit who gave it to you.

The Provider is also the One who Empowers!

While there are a variety of different options for television service out there now, many people still utilize their local cable television service. And, in many cases, whatever the cable TV service is, the home internet is also provided through the same company.

When a family gets set up in a house, apartment, condominium or living space, they contact the local cable company and sign up. That cable company then comes to the living space bringing electronic cable boxes, remote controls, control boxes for the wall, routers and sometimes even wireless networking equipment. Those service men for the cable company install the equipment and then get it all started working.

From that point on, the same company who provided the equipment also provides the signal and service to make it work. Day in and day out, the company still owns the equipment its customer is now using. Day in and day out, the company provides the signal so that the equipment will produce television, movies or internet signals – and sometimes telephone service.

In the same way the cable companies provide equipment then the service to make it work, the Holy Spirit does for every Christian. At conversion, the Holy Spirit sets up the "equipment" with His presence. That equipment is the gifts of the Spirit. From that day forward, the Holy Spirit also provides the signal and power that the equipment will function. Every spiritual gift we have as believers is owned by and empowered by the Holy Spirit.

What is our job? Stay moment by moment connected to and filled with the Holy Spirit!

FINAL THOUGHT: What is your plan daily to stay connected to the Word of God and to be in the correct posture to experience the filling of God?

DAY 5: The Exact, Precise Package I Need
1Corinthians 12:11
"All these are the work of one and the same Spirit, and he distributes them to each one, just as he determines."

Paul gives some insight into the distribution of the gifts of the Spirit. The "All these" are the complete inventory of spiritual gifts from which the Holy Spirit pulls when a person becomes born again. As the Holy Spirit pulls from "All these," He then distributes them according to how He determines.

Pulling from one inexhaustible inventory of spiritual gifts and channeling into the lives of millions of believers would seem an overwhelming task. And yet, the Holy Spirit does this effortlessly and without any glitches.

A person is never born again without then being personally supplied from this massive inventory of spiritual gifts.

A person is never born again without a personally customized supply of the correct spiritual gifts and enablement for glorifying Christ and edifying people.

A person is never born again without being sufficiently supplied from the vast inventory with every spiritual gift necessary for his or her victorious living.

Amazon carries over 600 million products to date. Each day, Amazon sells around 1 million products.

There are not many retailers that even begin to match the level of inventory that Amazon has. There are not many retailers that come close to matching the level of product shipment quantity that Amazon has.

How does Amazon know how to take their over 600 million products and place them in the exact type and quantity each person needs? It is because each customer orders what they want and how much they want. Amazon does not need to know what I want or need, or how much I want or need of an item, but they do need to be able place what I want in my possession.

No business, no matter how large or small, can determine what I want or need. The business must be told, so it can then put the products in the correct place from the inventory that they have.

With God, however, not only does He place the exact quantity and type of spiritual gift with each believer, He does it without the believers needing to order them.

The Holy Spirit is God! He pulls spiritual gifts from vast quantity of "All these" and "distributes them" with the correct people for glorifying Christ and edifying people. But, that placement is the Holy Spirit's choice. In his omniscience, He knows exactly what I need. He takes from His vast quantity to gifts and places it within me at conversion.

Look up, child of God! You have exactly what you need to serve God with the exact right amount to do what God is calling you to do.

FINAL THOUGHT: Prayerfully write down the areas you believe God might have given you to serve Him in your local church. Now, beside these areas, write down how you have gone about fulfilling these areas of calling.

The Perfect Counselor Study Guide: Week 8

1. As the Apostle Paul begins the explanation of the specific gifts of the Spirit, through what means does he say they are given? Why is that critical for every believer to know?

2. Read the following passages. For each passage, list the spiritual gifts that are mentioned.
    a. Romans 12:6-8
    b. 1Corinthians 12:8-10
    c. Ephesians 4:11
    d. 1Peter 4:11

3. Now, out beside each of the individual gifts of the Holy Spirit listed, note one place or ministry in your church where that gift could be utilized.

4. Paul emphasizes two important points in 1Corinthians 12:11 regarding the working of all the individual gifts of the Holy Spirit. One of these points relates to the unity of the gifts of the Holy Spirit and the other relates to the diversity of those same gifts. What are these two important points?

5. Read the following passages. Describe the different people in each passage and how their "spiritual gifts" distinctly contributed to the mission of Christ and the early church. Some of the passages may have more than one person. In those instances, describe each person. Try to be as specific as possible when describing each person's contribution to the Kingdom of God and the local church.

a. Mark 8:27-30 & Acts 1:15-16, 21-22
b. John 1:6-8
c. John 14:1-8
d. John 19:25-27
e. Acts 4:36-37
f. 1Corinthians 3:5-6
g. Philippians 2:19-24
h. Philippians 2:25-30

DAY 1: We Know the Owner

1Corinthians 12:28

"And God has appointed in the church first apostles, second prophets, third teachers, then miracles, then gifts of healing, helping, administrating, and various kinds of tongues."

As Paul describes how God enables His church to function through individual members, he also explains the enabling of those members. Each born again member of the local church body is equipped, or appointed, with an enablement to accomplish that which God desires us to do.

God, by His infinite wisdom, appoints the skills to each person as needed for that particular function. These functions serve to point people to Christ and strengthen the body of Christ. While the ministry functions are fulfilled within each born-again believer, God Himself appoints which skill is given to each believer.

Finding a Christian's strength has more to do with knowing God than with knowing those skills. Learning about the spiritual gifts God supplies is important, but knowing the God of those gifts is far more critical.

Imagine a little boy whose dad owns a restaurant in a large, bustling city. Suppose that restaurant is famous for its gourmet hamburgers and milkshakes. A lot of people daily go in and out of that restaurant talking about the wonderful hamburgers and milkshakes. They tell their friends about these tasty meals. The burgers and shakes are special for people to purchase. And yet, the little boy, whose dad owns the restaurant, gets to eat burgers and drink the tasty shakes almost whenever he wants. The little boy, more than knowing about the products, knows the owner of the products.

A believer who is familiar with the different kinds of spiritual gifts can be helpful in functioning and utilizing them. However, a believer knowing the God who appoints those gifts is far more important.

When I was in high school, the father of a friend of mine owned a local car dealership. Each of us guys drooled over the possibility of driving one of those new cars or trucks from that car lot. We knew about the types of cars, the engines they possessed and the paint colors that were placed on them. We knew about those cars. And yet, my friend – whose father owned the lot – drove multiple new cars. You see, we knew about the products, but his father owned the products. He had far more access to them.

The God of the universe has established certain spiritual gifts that He Himself appoints to each believer. Since He owns them and appoints them, knowing Him is the most critical piece of operating in those gifts.

Look up child of God! If you want to operate in the gifts God has and appoints, be sure to spend the most time knowing that God!

FINAL THOUGHT: Read through 1Corinthians 13, which is the love chapter. This is the motive and intent behind God's work for us. The function of God's appointed gifts is most effective when they operate by this heart of love.

DAY 2: The Proper Connection
1Corinthians 12:28
"And God has appointed in the church first apostles, second prophets, third teachers, then miracles, then gifts of healing, helping, administrating, and various kinds of tongues."

From Galatians, Ephesians, Philippians, and Colossians to Romans, 1Corinthians, and 2Corinthians and beyond, the Apostle Paul was clear in his writings about his love for the local church.

It was the Apostle Paul who wrote of the church being the bride of Christ (2Corinthians 11:2, Ephesians 5:25-33). He expressed the beauty of the local church.

It was the Apostle Paul who wrote of the local church as being the body of Christ (1Corinthians 12:12-14, Ephesians 4:1-16). He expressed the power and substance of the local church.

It was the Apostle Paul who wrote of the local church as being the temple of God (1Corinthians 3:16-17). He expressed the great and enormous value of the local church.

The Apostle Paul had an enormous love and care for the local church. And, as he described God's appointing of gifts and enablements, he explains that they are appointed in the church. These spiritual gifts and abilities God gives each believer to extend His Kingdom, equip His saints, and glorify His name are at work in the local church.

The church that is beautiful, powerful and valuable is where God chooses to equip His saints. And outside of the local church, a born-again Christian cannot fully access or fulfill his or her spiritual gifts. In the church is where God has chosen to bestow gifts and enable believers to function in these spiritual gifts. A Christian simply cannot claim to serve the Lord and yet not be a part of His local church. The spiritual gifts that God appoints are implemented within His church.

In our modern world of hand-held technology, besides the common ownership of smart phones, watches, and tablets, the only thing more commonly possessed are the chargers. Different electronic chargers have different tips for different pieces of equipment. Outwardly, it may seem that one charger is just as good as another. However, anyone who has ever had a smart phone with 2% charge and the wrong type of charger knows that the wrong charger connection offers no charge.

A charger cord with the proper tip offers the device an opportunity to have power. However, a smart phone with no charge, and a charger without the proper tip, becomes a paper weight or a doorstop. The key to effective electronics' usage is finding the correct charger connection.

When a person is saved, he or she is indwelt by the Holy Spirit and enabled with certain spiritual gifts. The use of these gifts happens effective in the context of the local church. God appoints these gifts in the church, and without that local church connection (i.e. charger tips), utilizing those spiritual gifts becomes ineffective and useless.

Look up, child of God! The Savior has given you a source and a place to fulfill the gifts appointed to you. Embrace and fulfill your role as a servant in God's church.

FINAL THOUGHT: Prayerfully consider how you are being used as a servant in a local church. If you are not currently participating in a local church, or you are and not serving, begin praying and asking God to show you how He might use you there

DAY 3: Stay Close to the Appointer
1Corinthians 12:29-30
"Are all apostles? Are all prophets? Are all teachers? Do all work miracles? [30] Do all possess gifts of healing? Do all speak with tongues? Do all interpret?"

The Apostle Paul poses seven consecutive questions in these two verses. All of these questions are related to how spiritual gifts were dispersed to the congregation in Corinth.

He wants to show how the gifts are appointed in the fellowship and whether or not everyone possesses all of these gifts. The questions are rhetorical. Paul knows the answer to them. None of these gifts – or offices – are possessed by every single person in the church. Quite the contrary. In fact, beyond that, it is true that, as sure as everyone does not possess all the gifts, no single person possesses every gift either.

In earlier verses, Paul explained the appointment of gifts that God made. He explained that God Himself gave gifts to each person in the fellowship by his own choosing and determination. It is this simple. God has a magnificent master plan for each local church. He knows exactly how many teachers, prophets, servants, administrators, workers of faith and pastors each local church requires.

Only God knows how the dispersion of gifts should go. Only God knows how many of each gift should go in each church. Only God knows which followers are to possess which abilities. Only God knows which enablement is to go to which person.

The greatest need of every believer is to spend quality time daily coming to know this God on a greater level. Knowing God on a deeper and more intimate level assures that we will be able to hear better from Him what gifts and abilities we are to fulfill.

In the past decade, companies that furnish drivers in their personal vehicles to provide transportation have grown exponentially. These transportation providers have drivers who drive around in their own, personal automobiles. As the drivers receive signals on their cell phones through an app, they accept driving assignments that are the closest to them. These drivers must stay close to their vehicles and close to their phones, or they will not know when and where they are being assigned to drive.

Many of these drivers do this business part time to go with their full-time occupation. Other drivers use this business as their primary income. However, in either case, if a driver wants to know his or her assignment, then he must stay close to the primary source that does the appointing. Getting disconnected from their cars or from their cell phone with the appointment app will cause the drivers to lose opportunities to pick up additional income.

In much the same way as these drivers work closely to the source of appointment, it is imperative for believers to stay close daily to the one who appoints us. God, in His great wisdom, appoints specific roles and ministries to specific people in the church. Getting disconnected or distant from our Savior will often result in missing out on opportunities to serve and bless.

Look up, child of God! He has a special appointment for you! Stay close daily and find out what it is!

FINAL THOUGHT: Write out your daily plan for spending time with the Lord in detail. Write down when it is, where it is, how long it lasts, and what you need for it to happen.

DAY 4: Our Primary Calling is the Best
1Corinthians 12:31
"But earnestly desire the higher gifts. And I will show you a still more excellent way."

The Apostle Paul surely wants the Corinthians to walk in their appropriate gifts. He has already let them know that not everyone possesses the same gift, and no one has all the gifts. Each person fulfills the role to which he or she is appointed by God and by the power of His Holy Spirit.

And still, even if a person becomes aware of where he is gifted, there could be an inappropriate motive. Paul seemed to tell the Corinthians that, while all gifts were critical, there were gifts that sat on a little higher level of priority than others. In fact, Paul called them to "earnestly desire" those gifts. That means to zealously want and pursue the gifts that are higher and greater. The confusing part is that he did not really reveal the higher and greater gifts.

Throughout the book of 1Corinthians, the Apostle was working on this group to see them use their gifts for God's glory and for one another. In other words, his priorities from the very beginning of this letter (such as 1Corinthians 1:10) were to bless God and bless one another with these spiritual gifts. In 1Corinthians 1:31, he calls them to "glory in the Lord" as they fulfill their callings. In 1Corinthians 3:23, he declares, "And you are Christ's, and Christ is God's."

What are these higher gifts? Based on the repeated call of Paul to care about God and about one another, one must assume that these higher gifts were any of the gifts used to primarily glorify God and edify believers. Using a spiritual gift to point to God and bless others in the fellowship is the highest way in which it may be used. Any gift – and every gift – has a highest purpose and other inferior purposes for which it can be used.

A screwdriver is effective to tighten a screw into its hole. This is its primary purpose. A screwdriver, at times, may also be used to tap a nail into wood. While this secondary use is the inferior and inefficient purpose, it can work.

A bucket with a handle is effective in carrying water from place to place. This is its primary use. Turned upside down, this bucket can become a place to sit. It is an uncomfortable and somewhat unstable place, but a place to sit, nevertheless.

A laptop computer can be effective in producing word processor documents, working on the internet, designing graphics or working online. This is the primary purpose of a laptop. A laptop, if positioned correctly, can also be used as an efficient doorstop. This could be a secondary purpose.

Every gift God appoints to each believer has a primary and highest calling - that of glorifying God and edifying other believers. Every spiritual gift can be used for secondary purposes, but the primary is glorifying God and edifying God's people.

God has called each and every believer to worship and serve in such a way that He is glorified and others are edified. If you are a born-again believer, God has enabled you with some spiritual gift – or gifts – that you might be used to glorify Him and strengthen other believers.

FINAL THOUGHT: Make a couple of notes of the areas where you believe God has enabled you to serve. In what ways can you see God glorified and others edified?

DAY 5: "A-GA-PE"
1Corinthians 12:31
"But earnestly desire the higher gifts. And I will show you a still more excellent way."

Paul extends his call from higher gifts to more excellent ones. The use of gifts for higher purposes is good, but utilizing gifts for excellent purposes is even better. In fact, some have said that the enemy of excellent is not bad, but the enemy of excellent is good. Would you settle for using your spiritual gifts for a good purpose when you could be using it for that which is excellent?

What then is the excellent about which the Apostle Paul speaks? For an answer to this, one must look into 1Corinthians 13. It is a chapter sandwiched in between 1Corinthians 12, which discusses spiritual gifts, and 1Corinthians 14, which discusses issues of tongues, prophets, and proper order in the public church service. Many know of 1Corinthians 13 as being "the love chapter." This is that chapter:

If I speak in the tongues of men and of angels, but have not love, I am a noisy gong or a clanging cymbal. [2] And if I have prophetic powers, and understand all mysteries and all knowledge, and if I have all faith, so as to remove mountains, but have not love, I am nothing. [3] If I give away all I have, and if I deliver up my body to be burned, but have not love, I gain nothing. [4] Love is patient and kind; love does not envy or boast; it is not arrogant [5] or rude. It does not insist on its own way; it is not irritable or resentful; [6] it does not rejoice at wrongdoing but rejoices with the truth. [7] Love bears all things, believes all things, hopes all things, endures all things. [8] Love never ends. As for prophecies, they will pass away; as for tongues, they will cease; as for knowledge, it will pass away. [9] For we know in part and we prophesy in part, [10] but when the perfect comes, the partial will pass away. [11] When I was a child, I spoke like a child, I thought like a child, I reasoned like a child. When I became a man, I gave up childish ways. [12] For now we see in a mirror dimly, but then face to face. Now I know in part; then I shall know fully, even as I have been fully known. [13] So now faith, hope, and love abide, these three; but the greatest of these is love.

Why would a chapter all about the power and purpose of love be sandwiched in between chapters on spiritual gifts and order in the church? The answer can be found in the word "excellent". Operating spiritual gifts and spiritual order in the local church are to be done in an excellent way, and that excellent way is with the motivating and inspiring power of love.

This love is a-ga-pe'. It is a love empowered by Christ Himself. Agape' is a love that is shown by the sacrificial act of Christ on the cross. Agape' is a love that cares more for the glory of God than for receiving for oneself. Agape' is a love that cares more for others than for oneself. Agape' is a love that pours oneself out for others with no assumption or expectation of anything in return. Agape' is a love that gives away but does not need to receive in order to keep giving. Agape' is a love that, at all costs, wants God the Father glorified by the Son through the power of the Holy Spirit!
Look up, child of God! Love with an agape' love. This is the excellent use of your spiritual gifts!

FINAL THOUGHT: Spend a few minutes meditating on 1Corinthians 13:4-8. As things cross your mind, make notes on how these elements of love might be seen in the exercise of spiritual gifts in the local church.

The Perfect Counselor Study Guide: Week 9

1. Read 1Corinthians 12:28 in 2-3 other translations besides the one you have. What words are used where it reads, "'And God has _____ in the church?'"

2. Is it significant for a local church to understand that those in leadership and utilizing spiritual gifts have been "appointed"? Explain why or why not.

3. Paul explains that the spiritual gifts appointed by God have been established "in the church".

   a. Why is it significant for believers to understand that these gifts are only "in the church"?

   b. Read through Romans 12:1-8. This passage begins with a life given completely to Christ. It concludes with an explanation of the individual spiritual gifts. That said, what would Romans 12:1 require as a minimum for a person to possess gifts of the Holy Spirit?

4. In 1Corinthians 12:29-30 the Apostle Paul poses seven questions. Read each of these questions carefully. These are essentially rhetorical questions (Hint: Paul already knows the answers). What point is Paul trying to make in making these rhetorical questions?

5. As Paul writes in 1Corinthians 12:31, he makes a declaration to every Christian. What does he call each Christian to do regarding gifts?

6. The final statement in 1Corinthians 12:31 is an invitation by Paul. What is the way he claims to want to show Christians?

7. The final statement of 1Corinthians 12:31 is essentially an introduction to 1Corinthians 13. Read 1Corinthians 13:1-13. Based on this passage that Paul explains as "the more excellent way", consider these questions:

    a. What is the more excellent way?

    b. Explain how "the more excellent way" could relate to these spiritual gifts.

THE PERFECT COUNSELOR DEVOTIONS: WEEK 10
Alone with God

DAY 1: Steady Wins!
Acts 2:42
"And they devoted themselves to the apostles' teaching and the fellowship, to the breaking of bread and the prayers."

Dr. Luke's reference to "they", in this case, is speaking of the followers of Christ – thousands of them brand new. According to Acts 2:41, "about three thousand souls" were saved. The fact that there were "about 3,000" suggests that there were probably even more than that.

What does a brand-new faith do when it suddenly gains more than 3,000 new followers – all at one time? According to this verse, what the leadership chose to do with these new believers was done regularly. The word "devoted" is a verb tense which means ongoing activity. They continued steadfastly or continually devoted themselves to that which was necessary to prepare 3,000 new believers for worshipping, loving, and serving Christ.

The disciplines and actions which go to making believers stronger and more mature are not one-time events, or even a handful of activities, but are the little things done day to day to day. If you are to grow, it will be a lot about what you do daily over a long period of time.

An article on the Army.com website from 2016 was titled" Exercise Consistency is the Key." The article contends:

Consistency in working out will bring more substantial results than periodic extreme fitness routines. Working out three hours a day for one month can bring on health problems including stress fractures, tendon and muscle strains that often discourage people from continuing to work out. Try slowly increasing work out time weekly or biweekly starting with 30 minutes, three times a week and slowly making it to 60 minutes five times a week.

Physical exercise is most effective for the human body when it is consistent over a long period of time. A person cannot suddenly get into good physical shape in one week or one month.

In the same way, spiritual growth is done as we participate in spiritual growth by the Holy Spirit in our lives as we "continue steadfastly". Your spiritual growth will not happen in a week, a month, or even a few months, but it will happen daily and over a period of time.

FINAL THOUGHT: Write out here some thoughts about your plan for daily continuing steadfastly in spiritual growth as it relates to prayer and God's Word.

DAY 2: All Believers. Each Activity. Regular Occurrence.
Acts 2:42
"And they devoted themselves to the apostles' teaching and the fellowship, to the breaking of bread and the prayers."

Luke recounted the activities that were a part of the ongoing ministry of the first local church. There were more than 3,000 people who were part of the initial church in Jerusalem. There were more than 3,000 people who had been converted and had become part of the first church. The more than 3,000 men, women and children needed to be encouraged, discipled, and directed on how to live the Christian life. What could the church leaders do to make those things happen?

According to the initial descriptions of this first church, there were several activities that were regular and ongoing that helped to disciple God's people and grow His fellowship. These activities included:

- <u>TEACHING:</u> This word refers to system instruction. This instruction was precept by precept and point by point done with the intention of growing God's people spiritually.

- <u>FELLOWSHIP:</u> This word koi-no-ni-a in this context is not a verb, but it is a noun. The people were devoted, not so much to fellowshipping, but to the fellowship. They were devoted to the gathered body of people. Being together with the other believers was critical to them.

- <u>BREAKING OF BREAD:</u> This behavior involved fellowship feasts together. These community meals were often called "love feasts." They usually involved an observance of the Lord's Supper/Communion.

- PRAYERS: This is the most general and often used term for prayer in the New Testament. In this context, it is speaking of consistent, ongoing corporate prayer of all types.

It is amazing that, with more than 3,000 new converts, the leadership of the church believed that being involved in these four basic activities was the key to discipling them. And, still today, teaching the Scriptures (and being taught), consistently being a part of the fellowship of a local church, gathering to worship and the Lord's Supper and praying is still a key in spiritual growth.

These events are part of the key and participating in them "steadfastly" is the other part. Born-again believers must be in consistent, ongoing, repeated involvement with other born-again believers in a local church through teaching, gathering, eating, praying, and observing the Lord's Supper if they desire to grow spiritually.

FINAL THOUGHT: Think back over the last 2-3 months of your life. Could you honestly say that your involvement in a local church has consistently included these four areas? Can you honestly say that you have experienced these four areas in a local church on a regular, ongoing basis? Finally, if every person in your local church participated in these experiences with the schedule that you do, what kind of spiritual maturity would your church honestly possess?

DAY 3: It's Awesome!
Acts 2:43
"And awe came upon every soul, and many wonders and signs were being done through the apostles."

As Luke wrote about the beginnings and the launching of the early church, he described the regular, weekly activities. He described the teaching, the worship, the fellowship and the prayers. He described the gathering of the fellowship around the Lord's Supper table. He even (earlier in the chapter) described the celebration of baptism.

All of these activities are what might be considered regular and normal ongoing services and activities of the church. And yet, in the midst of regular church meetings, it is explained that "awe came upon every soul". This awe was not in response to some special events or some spectacularly scheduled services. This awe was in response to the regular, daily and weekly gatherings of this early group of believers.

When the church gathers, a group of people are all together in one place who have been baptized into the Holy Spirit of God. And, if all – or even most – of those people are filled and controlled in those moments by the Holy Spirit, imagine the power that is being expressed in one meeting? The One who spoke the universe into existence in six days is showing up through every believer in that meeting. The One who parted the Red Sea for the Israelites to cross over on dry land shows up through every believer in that meeting. The One who raised Lazarus from the dead shows up through every believer in that meeting.

When that kind of power and presence shows up in a gathering of people, would it not be expected that awesome things will take place? When that kind of power and presence shows up in a gathering of men, women, boys and girls, would it not be expected that awesome things will erupt? In fact, if that kind of an awesome presence shows up among a room of gathered people, and awesome things do not happen, then something is wrong.

Which brings us to this question: When we are gathered together with our church, should there not be a sense of awe there regularly? Granted, some meetings might be more powerful and impactful than others. But if the very Creator of the Universe and the fourth man in the fire (Daniel 3:24-26), shows up in and through God's people in a gathering of God's church, then powerful, awesome things will naturally happen.

What part do you have to play in those potentially awesome meetings? It all depends how much the Holy Spirit is filling you as you gather with your fellowship. In fact, if everyone in your church gathering were filled by the Holy Spirit the way you are, then how powerful would things be? In preparation for an awesome service and gathering at your church, seek to walk intimately with Jesus, and come into these gatherings powerfully controlled by His Holy Spirit.

And when many – or most – of God's people gather with His Spirit controlling them, His awesome presence will permeate the atmosphere. If His presence is to permeate, then it will at least mean He is permeating you.

FINAL THOUGHT: Think of ways that you might spiritually prepare yourself for the next gathering of your church family. List some of those thoughts and prepare to do them prior to your next meeting.

DAY 4: The Heightened Senses of the Church
Acts 2:44
"And all who believed were together and had all things in common."

As the description of the early church continued to grow, and as Luke continued the description of those gathered meetings, he included activity outside of them as well. The interconnectivity of that first church was powerful and visible.

The unity involved much more than just good feelings. It involved the practical sharing of material and physical possessions. This sharing was done in a way that met the basic needs of any members who had them. The sharing was done as a matter of course and did not require a specific, dedicated ministry to motivate the generosity.

This early church contained a basic level of organization – minus church staff or associates. In that respect, it looked much different than many current churches. However, the concepts of ongoing empathy toward the needs of other believers and making one's personal possessions available to be shared is still a constant calling of the church of Jesus Christ. THE CONCEPT OF SHARING OUR TIME, TALENT, AND RESOURCES WITH EACH OTHER IN THE CHURCH HAS NOT CHANGED!

If a body is operating at peak efficiency, then when one part of that body is in need, the other parts naturally step in to help. In a body operating effectively, this move to help parts in need is a natural response without a lot of thought. This is true with the spiritual body that is the church and the physical body.

In a March 2017 online article in Live Science titled "Why Other Senses May Be Heightened in Blind People", a study on the non-sight senses of blind people was examined. What many have suspected was found to be verified scientifically:

> The people who were blind had fewer connections between the visual parts of the brain and other areas of the brain," compared with the people who were not blind, Bauer said.

But 'there are also areas of the brain, associated with other senses, that are more interconnected', such as areas involved with language and auditory processing, she said. By strengthening the connections among these areas, it appears that brain may be compensating for blindness, she said.

When a person goes blind, the other four senses begin to sharpen and increase. The neurotransmitters in the brain often will increase in the other areas of the senses as they decrease relative to sight.

The body will tend to grow stronger in some areas to support the sectors which have weakened. And so, the spiritual Body of Christ. Those in Christ who have more are motivated to help those who do not. This is part of the joy and fellowship of the church.

FINAL THOUGHT: Take a moment and write down the areas where you are giving and/or serving, so that your strength in those areas helps and upholds those who may be weaker: In financial resources, In biblical knowledge, In available time, In knowledge of family, In physical health, etc.

DAY 5: Christian, You Need the Groups...Large and Small
Acts 2:46-47
"And day by day, attending the temple together and breaking bread in their homes, they received their food with glad and generous hearts, praising God and having favor with all the people. And the Lord added to their number day by day those who were being saved."

Luke added yet another commentary on the state and progress of the first church. As the church consistently taught, fellowshipped, worshipped, prayed, and gathered, the impact within the church and in the community was profound.

First, even as the church grew, the believers consistently continued to gather together in a large group ("attending the temple") and in small group gatherings ("in their homes"). The early church began the pattern for the church for all time that both large, main group gatherings and small group gatherings are necessary for the health and growth of the church.

Every church should have, as its normal, ongoing pattern, gatherings that include the whole fellowship together for exhortation and worship. In addition, every church should have an ongoing pattern of small group gatherings for ministry, fellowship, instruction, and outreach. This schedule of gathering is the prototype for all local churches. These different types of regular gatherings are necessary for the health, growth, and ministry of the church.

No church should only choose either the large group worship or the small group gatherings. Rather, every church should choose both.

The same is true for each Christian family and each believer. The involvement of a believer in the church should involve large, main group worship gatherings. Each Christian family or individual should also be sure to be a part of a small group Bible study or small group gathering.

The encouragement, learning, and exhortation of the gathered church is necessary for you to grow and be helped as a believer. The opportunity to encourage others is necessary for you in the large group gathering.

In the same way, as a believer and member of a local church, you have a great need to connect with a small group. In the small group, you gain a greater intimacy with other believers. In the small group, you have greater opportunities to interact over Scripture. In the small group you have more opportunities to experience daily life with other believers in ways that will support them and allow them to support you.

When the Holy Spirit oversees your church, both large group worship and small group ministry will happen effectively. When the Holy Spirit oversees your family, both large group worship and small group ministry will be a part of your weekly involvement. When the Holy Spirit oversees your life, both large group worship and small group ministry will be part of your regular, weekly schedule.

FINAL THOUGHT: Make two lists. In one list, write down ways in which you can minister to others in your main worship services in your church. Whether they are Saturday nights, Sunday mornings, Sunday nights, Wednesday nights – or some other time – how can you minister to others during these times? Next, make a list of ways in which you can bless and minister to others in your small group gatherings.

The Perfect Counselor Study Guide: Week 10

In the passage in Acts 2:42-46, the church begins. As that first church begins under the power and baptism of the Holy Spirit, His activities, events, and expressions are seen through that church. As you work through these following questions, consider how they represent the signature of the Holy Spirit on the early church.

1. According to Acts 2:42, in the introductory phrase, how often did the early church perform the activities described in this verse? (Hint: Consulting several different translations will help here).

2. There are four activities mentioned of the early church in Acts 2:42. Below list those four activities.

3. Consult the four activities you have listed from the previous question, in 2-3 sentences, explain what each of these did to build and grow that early church – and your own local church.

   a. Apostles' teaching:

   b. The Fellowship:

   c. Breaking of bread:

   d. Prayers:

4. According to Acts 2:43, what was the impact of the local church ministry on each individual of that time?

5. Specifically, according to Acts 2:43, through whom were the wonders and signs performed?

6. A sign is a statement that points in the direction of the thing it is highlighting. If the apostles were performing signs, then these signs were pointing to the main destination. Where would these signs, performed by the apostles, be pointing?

7. According to Acts 2:44, what was another key characteristic of that early church?

8. Acts 2:46 describes two distinct locations of gatherings. Take a moment and list each one.

9. These two types of gatherings included a large, corporate worship service and a small group gathering. Which was which?

10. With all of the church ministry and activity, the last phrase of Acts 2:47 describes what outcomes?

ENDORSEMENTS

"The Perfect Counselor is an excellent devotional! Dr. Johnny Ellison exegetes each biblical passage while simultaneously addressing its theological implications before making life applications through the usage of relevant illustrations. Dr. Ellison does this while still making the devotional easy to understand and live-out with the help of his application centered questions. I admire Dr. Ellison's faithfulness to the text in the composition of this great devotional. If you are searching for a devotion, I highly recommend The Perfect Counselor"!

-JJ Washington, Georgia Baptist Mission Board, West Central Region Consultant

"All of us are in need of some spiritual B12 vitamins and Pastor Johnny Ellison has helped provide that prescription for us. In this brief, but poignant series of Bible studies, you will discover new truths about our Perfect Counselor.

As I read these studies, like John Wesley of old, my heart was strangely warmed, and I felt a real sense of the presence of God with me. I pray the same experience will be yours as you utilize this impactful series of Bible studies as personal devotionals and/or in small groups of people who want to go deeper into the Word.

I highly recommend Perfect Counselor. You will be blessed by this study. Pastor Johnny Ellison is to be commended for a job well done in rightly dividing the Word."

-Christmas Blessings,
Rick Lance Executive Director Alabama Baptist State Board of Missions
John 15:5

"The Perfect Counselor" is an amazing guide and companion to anyone wanting to "keep in step with the Spirit" in their daily life! Dr. Johnny Ellison has done an amazing job taking the scriptures on one of the most misunderstood parts of the New Testament and making them something understandable bet yet powerful. From great stories from history to great examples of day to day living, this book could serve as a daily devotion, small group study and guide or a sermon series for Pastors! I am blessed to have read this work and I am excited for you to do so as well!"

-Mike Linch
Senior Pastor NorthStar Church
Host of the "Linch with a Leader" Podcast

The Perfect Counselor is the perfect study, if you hunger to know God's voice and leading better in your life.

My friend, Dr. Johnny Ellison has provided a well-designed, highly insightful, user friendly" study of the person and the work of the Holy Spirit that is sure to make a difference in a life that seeks God.
Each lesson carefully builds upon a previous one in depth and development to a Strong faith.

Dr. Ellison hits the target by reminding us that when He, the Holy Spirit, is in relationship with us, Gods children, we find the abundant, fruitful, & fulfilling Christian life we read about in scripture!

-Bill Purvis senior Pastor Cascade Hills Church, Columbus, Ga

I was blessed beyond my expectations to begin reading this Devotional called, "The Perfect Counselor." Using it every day is the equivalent of taking a pill daily that helps us become more physically healthy and strong. Following this daily Devotional will provide you with a consistent injection of God's Word that will help transform your life.

Romans 12:2 (NKJV)
² And do not be conformed to this world, but be transformed by the renewing of your mind, that you may prove what *is* that good and acceptable and perfect will of God.

-Dr. Michael D. Woods
President MWE Ministry School
Pastor and Seminary Instructor

Made in the USA
Monee, IL
25 February 2020

22278999R00075